MW00623062

THOMAS MERTON, LAWRENCE FERLINGHETTI, AND THE PROTECTION OF ALL BEINGS:

THE CORRESPONDENCE

BY BILL MORGAN

PUBLISHED BY BEATDOM BOOKS

Published by Beatdom Books

Copyright © 2022 by Bill Morgan

All rights reserved. No part of this book may be reproduced
in any form or by any electronic or mechanical means
including information storage and retrieval systems, without
permission in writing from the author. The only exception is
by a reviewer, who may quote short excerpts in a review.

View the publisher's website:
www.beatdom.com

Printed in the United Kingdom
First Print Edition
ISBN 978-0-9934099-9-8

Copyright Information

The letters of Lawrence Ferlinghetti: Copyright Estate of Lawrence Ferlinghetti

"Original Child Bomb": By Thomas Merton, from *The Collected Poems of Thomas Merton*, copyright 1962 by The Abbey of Gethsemani. Reprinted by permission of New Directions Publishing Corp.

"Chant to Be Used in Processions Around a Site with Furnaces": By Thomas Merton, from *The Collected Poems of Thomas Merton*, copyright 1963 by The Abbey of Gethsemani, Inc., 1977 by The Trustees of the Merton Legacy Trust. Reprinted by permission of New Directions Publishing Corp.

The letters of Thomas Merton: Reprinted by permission of New Directions Publishing Corp.

For Bill Keogan (1947-2022)
St. John's University Librarian and Friend of
Scholars Everywhere

Acknowledgements

Many people helped make this book possible. First and foremost, I'd like to thank Lawrence Ferlinghetti, who was a friend for more than 50 years. The idea for this book was born out of early conversations with him and I'm sorry that he didn't live to see the result.

Without the enthusiastic and generous help of Dr. Paul M. Pearson, the director of the Thomas Merton Center at Bellarmine University, this book would never have gotten off the ground. He tirelessly answered my many questions and guided me to important sources. He was the person who discovered that Merton had actually taken photographs while staying in Ferlinghetti's North Beach apartment and allowed me to use them as illustrations.

Of equal importance was the help of Nancy Peters, long-time editor and co-owner of City Lights Books. Without her the idea would never have developed into a book. As Lawrence's literary executor she provided permission to use his work and willingly read the manuscript in its infancy. Nancy has always been a valuable resource for many of my projects and I owe her more than I can ever express here.

Christopher Wait at New Directions Publishing paved the way for permission to use Merton's words and countless librarians provided support along the way. Letters by Merton, Ferlinghetti, and Laughlin are preserved in the special collections units of Bellarmine University, the University of California at Berkeley, Harvard University, and Stanford University.

Much-needed photo help came from Peter Hale at the Allen Ginsberg Trust, the Larry Keenan Estate, and the Thomas Merton Center.

Early on *Beatdom* publisher David S. Wills saw the importance of this book and took the time to edit it carefully. His work throughout the whole Covid pandemic helped produce the handsome edition you hold in your hands. His technical and editorial mastery was crucial and was provided when it was most needed.

And finally, a special thanks to my wife and best friend, Judy Matz. Her steadfast love, encouragement, and support of this and other projects throughout the past 40 years has made it all worthwhile.

Lawrence Ferlinghetti, 1965. Copyright Larry Keenan.

Photograph of Thomas Merton by Sibylle Akers. Used with Permission of the Merton Legacy Trust and the Thomas Merton Center at Bellarmine University.

One afternoon while Lawrence Ferlinghetti and I were lingering over lunch at the old U.S. Restaurant on Columbus Avenue in San Francisco's North Beach, we found ourselves talking about Thomas Merton. The U.S. was one of Lawrence's favorite restaurants and every time we stopped there he told me the same story – that the U.S. didn't stand for the United States, but instead stood for "Unione Sportiva," a group of Italian sports teams that once thrived in that old Italian neighborhood of San Francisco. How the conversation turned towards writers and Thomas Merton in particular I'll never be able to remember, but it did. Ferlinghetti told me that he had known Merton and that when "Father Louis" (as he was known within the church community) had flown to Asia on what was to be his final trip, he had stayed overnight at the City Lights apartment. "I took him to the airport and that was the last anyone ever saw of him," Lawrence said, referring to the fact that Merton had died accidentally in Thailand of a fatal electrical shock not long afterwards.

Lawrence's memory wasn't exactly accurate, or more likely he wasn't allowing the facts to get in the way of a good story. His version was more dramatic than the actual story, but it intrigued me at the time and I asked him about his relationship with Merton several times over the following years. I could tell that Ferlinghetti admired Merton as both a writer and as a man and it was always interesting to discover who Lawrence's heroes were.

Decades later, I still found myself thinking about their relationship and how odd it seemed to me that these two men had become friends. Amid the Covid-19 pandemic in early 2021, I broached the subject of writing a book on the friendship between Merton and Ferlinghetti with Nancy Peters, Lawrence's closest friend, business partner, and confidante. Nancy was the one person who Ferlinghetti always deferred to on editorial matters during the fifty years I had known him. At the time, Lawrence was bedridden and could barely see, so I wanted to check with her before I said anything to him on the phone. Soon after I wrote to her, she spoke with Ferlinghetti and asked him what he thought about the idea. He replied that it seemed "Wonderful." Sadly, he passed away a few weeks later – just before his 102nd birthday – and I never had a chance to talk to him again. I felt that through his single word, he had given me the approval I needed to pursue the topic.

Initially, I believed that there was little in common between the two men. True, they were both poets and writers, but one had lived a monastic life for more than twenty-five years and died at a relatively young age, while the other had described himself as an anarchist and an international gadfly who lived to be more than a hundred. Ferlinghetti delighted in intentionally provoking the establishment by criticizing and challenging nearly every existing convention in America. By contrast, Merton always endeavored to obey the dictates of his Trappist superiors and strove to adhere to orthodox Catholic doctrine as strictly as he could. As I became more involved in my research, I came to understand that these outward differences belied underlying similarities.

Ferlinghetti first heard of Thomas Merton when the monk's book, *The Seven Storey Mountain*, became an unexpected best seller late in 1948. When the book first came out, no one, except maybe his editor, Robert Giroux, expected it to stay on the best sellers list for years, sell more than a million copies, and be proclaimed as one of the greatest books of the century. Who would imagine that an autobiography of a thirty-one-year-old, cloistered Trappist monk could have any impact on the world? Surprisingly, at that same time in the late forties, Lawrence recalled that he was reading St. Augustine, Thomas Aquinas, and a lot of Catholic literature. He had just returned to America from France, where on one occasion he had visited the Benedictines at the Solesmes Abbey and had become particularly interested in Trappist discipline and their way of life. "[Merton] was probably the first modern Catholic writer that I had ever read... I identified with him quite strongly," Lawrence told film-maker Paul Wilkes in an interview.

Both Merton and Ferlinghetti had roots deep in France. Thomas Merton had been born there in 1915, making him just a few years older than Lawrence. Although Lawrence had been born in Yonkers in 1919, he had been taken to France as a baby and raised there by his aunt. He learned to speak French before English, one of many things the two writers had in common. Ferlinghetti's father died before Lawrence was born and his mother was committed to a sanitarium shortly after his birth. Merton's mother died when he was six years old and his father passed away in 1931, just before Thomas' sixteenth birthday. As a result, both boys had been essentially orphaned and were shuffled from place to place, each growing up with no real sense of security or roots. In the introduction to *Thomas Merton and James Laughlin: Selected Letters*, editor David D. Cooper points out that as a boy Merton was a ward and an "object of charitable concern." Those same words could easily describe Ferlinghetti. After returning to the United States as a young boy, Lawrence was abandoned by his aunt on the doorstep of a wealthy family who raised him as a charity case. While growing up, both boys had their share of run-ins. A friend recently reported that his mother had known Merton in college and was quick to mention that "he was no saint." Ferlinghetti was no saint either, and one of his favorite stories was that he had been arrested for shoplifting the same week he was made an Eagle Scout.

After spending an unproductive year at Clare College in Cambridge, Merton relocated to New York City and enrolled at Columbia College in the winter of 1935. By coincidence, Ferlinghetti would also attend Columbia but not before finishing his undergraduate studies at the University of North Carolina. After his World War II service in the Navy, Lawrence was discharged and attended Columbia on the GI Bill, where he earned his master's degree in English literature in 1947, enabling him to continue his studies at the Sorbonne in Paris, graduating with a PhD in 1950. There he began to study Catholicism. In an interview with Barry Silesky, his biographer, Ferlinghetti stated that "If you live in Paris, you can become completely entranced by the aesthetic of the Gothic, the aesthetic of Catholicism..." He went on to say that "The whole aesthetic of the Gothic church has a very powerful effect, even if you're not interested in theology. The Catholics weren't dumb when they used incense and the Latin mass and organ music. It's like an ancient magic. You can become completely wrapped up in the aesthetic without being persuaded by the theology of it at all." He made friends with a Jesuit priest and they had frequent, often heated discussions about Catholic doctrine. For Ferlinghetti, it was a period of great discovery and intellectual stimulation.

By the time Ferlinghetti entered the Sorbonne in the late forties, Merton had already finished his academic work. He had earned his degree from Columbia in English literature and had begun graduate work focusing on the poetry of William Blake. In 1938, a friend, Dr. Bramachari, had suggested to Merton that he read *The Confessions of St. Augustine* and this combined with his Blake studies helped fuel an interest in a spiritual life and in Roman Catholicism in particular. In *The Seven Storey Mountain*, Merton explained the importance of his Blake studies in his decision to become a monk:

> The Providence of God was eventually to use Blake to awaken something of faith and love in my own soul – in spite of all the misleading notions, and all the almost infinite possibilities of error that underlie his weird and violent figures. I do not, therefore, want to seem to canonize him. But I have to acknowledge my own debt to him, and the truth which may appear curious to some, although it is really not so: that through Blake I would one day come, in a round-about way, to the only true Church, and to the One Living God, through His Son, Jesus Christ.

The following year, Merton decided to join the Franciscans, but he felt he didn't quite fit into the Franciscan world and so, after teaching for a year at St. Bonaventure University, he turned to the Trappists instead. In 1941, a few days after the Japanese attack on Pearl Harbor, Thomas Merton entered the Abbey of Our Lady of Gethsemani in Kentucky, where he remained until his death. By contrast, a few months earlier, Ferlinghetti had enlisted in the Navy, where he was to spend the duration of the war, a period that was to dramatically shape his future worldview.

Following his graduations from Columbia and then the Sorbonne, Ferlinghetti knocked around Europe for a while before returning to the United States. He discovered San Francisco in 1951, a town that reminded him of those gleaming, bright towns on the Mediterranean coast. When he first arrived, he moved into a boarding house with a French name, the Chateau Bleu, but he recalled that it was "very un-French." While living there, he continued work on an experimental novel he was writing. To his future wife, Kirby Selden-Smith, he wrote:

> I type all day. And what is it the morally-repugnant, mentally-marinated weakling is typing? A novel. About what is this novel? Paris and two or three people in Paris. (Are they aware of the existence of Evil? Yes, in fact, very sentiently they are aware). Who are they? Two men, one woman. The men, ex-novices from a Trappist Monastery – who did not find the kind of 'sanctuary' in the twittering world. One of them, the fine, flute-handled hero – a kind of Stephen Daedalus warmed-up and seen in his Paris days... and our fine foundering, wandering hero finding in earthly love his sanctuary; and so kiss kiss kiss. Encompassing the problem of the Christian versus the non-Christian Contemplative Ideal (cf. Charles Morgan, *The Fountain*; Merton, *Seven Stories to a Mountain* [sic]; *Ulysses*), all showing me to be the doubtful (doubting) Thomist I seem primarily to be.

To pay his bills, Ferlinghetti found a part-time job teaching French and after a while he began to teach English literature at the University of San Francisco, a Catholic Jesuit college. He needed an income to support his new wife, whom he had courted in France, but his real aspiration was to become a painter. One day in 1953, while walking home from his studio, he happened upon a man named Peter Martin, who was

5

starting a bookstore on Columbus Avenue in North Beach. Martin had the idea of opening an all-paperback bookstore, but he needed a partner and so, for an investment of $500, Ferlinghetti became the co-owner of the City Lights Pocket Book Store. Before long, Martin became homesick for New York City and Lawrence bought out his share of the business. It was then that he decided that he would publish books as well as sell them. In addition to his painting, Lawrence, in the French tradition, had pursued other art forms as well. He had been writing novels and poetry and so the first book that City Lights was to publish was his own collection of poems, which he called *Pictures of the Gone World*. This book drew the attention of the head of New Directions, James Laughlin, by then a friend and publisher of Thomas Merton for more than a decade.

James Laughlin was born into the wealthy Laughlin family of Pittsburgh, who owned the giant Jones & Laughlin Steel Corporation. J, as he was known to his friends, was not interested in the steel industry, but instead wanted to become a poet. In the 1930s, he visited Italy to meet and talk to the expatriate American poet, Ezra Pound. Pound, the great editor and friend of James Joyce, Ernest Hemingway, and T.S. Eliot, was just the person to determine whether his poetry had potential. In another case of not letting the truth get in the way of a good story, Laughlin always claimed that Pound had told him "You're never going to be a good poet, why don't you take up something useful instead?"[1] In the future, this story would be referred to as the "origin myth" by the staff at the New Directions publishing company. Even if it wasn't directly at Pound's suggestion, Laughlin decided that if he couldn't write great poetry, he could at least use some of the family fortune to publish great works. Beginning in 1936, New Directions began to release volume after volume of challenging, modern poetry that no other commercial publisher would handle. In 1944, well before Merton became

---

[1] Fox, Peggy L. "James Laughlin and Thomas Merton: 'Louie, I Think This Is The Beginning Of A Beautiful Friendship'" (in) The Merton Annual, no. 26 (2013) pp. 12-23.

James Laughlin. Copyright Allen Ginsberg Estate.

famous with the release of *The Seven Storey Mountain,* Laughlin published Tom's first collection, *Thirty Poems,* which was followed in 1946 by *A Man In The Divided Sea.* Initially, Laughlin heard about Merton through Mark Van Doren, who had been Tom's literature professor at Columbia. In 1943, Van Doren gave J a small collection of poems by the recently cloistered monk who had once been one of his favorite students. In part due to Van Doren's enthusiasm, Laughlin disregarded the traditional style of the poems and read deeper into the meaning behind his overtly religious and accessible words. J had been experiencing his own spiritual emptiness and the freshness of Merton's faith appealed to him.

This yearning to discover a spiritual basis for life also drove the philosophical pursuits of many of the nascent Beat Generation writers. Indeed, it was what had taken Ferlinghetti to visit the abbey in France while he was studying in Paris and the same spiritual quest lies beneath the early writings of many of the Beat writers. To over-simplify, Ferlinghetti, Allen Ginsberg, Jack Kerouac, Gary Snyder, Michael McClure, Philip Whalen, and many others were searching for a belief on which to anchor their lives in the post-war era.

It is remarkable that Mark Van Doren was the professor who was instrumental in the early development of not just Thomas Merton, but also Lawrence Ferlinghetti, Jack Kerouac, and Allen Ginsberg, each of whom studied under him during their times at Columbia. Each of them left college with a yearning for an undiscovered spiritual center to their lives. As Merton later wrote, "It was the only place where I ever heard anything really sensible said about any of the things that were really fundamental – life, death, time, love, sorrow, fear, wisdom, suffering, eternity." If Merton found what he was looking for in the quiet solitude of the Abbey of Gethsemani, the others searched further afield in the greater world. It was J Laughlin, in part through his gifts of newly published books to Merton, who influenced Merton to become more active in the big issues of the country and the world. Eventually, Tom Merton would work hard to help solve the problems of the world outside the monastery. Civil rights, war resistance, and the environment were issues that became a focus of much of Merton's later writing. To satisfy Merton's desire to keep abreast of new, avant garde literature, Laughlin began to send boxes of books by New Directions authors directly to the monastery, which, after passing the censors, found their way onto his reading table. Thus, unlikely books for a monk, such as works by Franz Kafka, Henry Miller, and Albert Camus, became part of Merton's lexicon. He defended his wide range of reading material by saying that those in the monastery should "know more about the injustices of the outside world and its problems. What good was prayer if you didn't know what to pray for?" Laughlin was repaid by Merton's spiritual guidance during his own times of crises later on.

It was in 1958 that New Directions published Ferlinghetti's *A Coney Island of the Mind,* a collection of poems that would go on to sell well over a million copies. Laughlin wanted to share this new discovery with Merton but was afraid that Ferlinghetti's irreverent style might offend the censors at the monastery. The Trappist administrators had the right to approve or disapprove of any books coming into the monastery, so there was a layer of censorship that had to be navigated. Even Merton's own poetry and prose had to be submitted for their approval before it could be sent to Laughlin or any other publisher, so J cautiously wrote Merton asking if he might send along a copy of *Coney Island.* Merton wrote back saying, "Larry Ferlinghetti's stuff sounds interesting. I now have permission to read anything so there are no problems about the nature of the material... Am interested in everything that is alive, and anything that strikes you as something I ought to know about, please send." In the same letter, Merton wrote "On the whole I think a monastery is not ordinarily a place to write good verse in. Too much triviality is dictated by the walls." So he was obviously eager to see what was being written in the outside world and use it to inform his own writing. It was part of his move from the cloistered world he was living in to the wider world outside the four walls of Gethsemani Abbey. In a letter to his friend, the South American poet Nicanor Parra, Merton wrote: "Today the poets and other artists tend to fulfill many of the functions that were once the monopoly of monks – and which of course the monks have made haste to abandon."

Ferlinghetti's poetry spoke to Merton's need for something new and it helped Tom develop his own unique response to matters of national and international importance. Along with the writings of activist priests like Daniel and Philip Berrigan, Ferlinghetti's work addressed the great miscarriages of justice of the day. Beginning with his poems "Tentative Description Of A Dinner To Promote the Impeachment Of President Eisenhower" and "One Thousand Fearful Words For Fidel Castro," Lawrence was confronting the issues of the day through a much more accessible form of poetry. These examples must have had some effect on Merton because by the late 1950s his poetry was becoming much more outspoken on a variety of similar topics.

One of Merton's lifelong friends, the poet Robert Lax, was also a product of Columbia College and another of Mark Van Doren's pupils who went on to have a long and impressive literary career. Merton wrote of his professor, "Not all of us took his courses ... yet nevertheless our common respect for Mark's sanity and wisdom did much to make us aware of how much we ourselves had in common." Lax was also a friend of Kerouac and Ginsberg and a practitioner of meditation and spiritual discipline, to the point of being known as a bit of a hermit himself. This desire to live a life of meditation is common to many writers. Kerouac in particular always dreamed of getting away to a secluded retreat where he could become closer to God. He envisioned a cabin in the woods where he would be able to restore his soul, which had been battered by the pressure of celebrity. Eastern religions such as Buddhism either replaced or supplemented Catholicism for many of these writers. In addition to Lax, poets like Gary Snyder, Philip Whalen, and even Ginsberg spent long periods on Buddhist meditation retreats. At one point, sensing that they had many things in common, Merton wrote to Lax asking him to bring Kerouac down to meet him at the monastery. Unfortunately, that meeting never took place. In 1960, Merton suggested that Laughlin bring Ferlinghetti along on one of J's frequent visits to Gethsemani. Although these visits never happened, it illustrates that Merton was open to meeting the

Beat poets and wanted to discuss many of the things they had in common. Gary Snyder, whose study of Buddhism was as intense as Merton's Catholicism, was the only one of the group who actually made the trip to Kentucky to see Thomas. Snyder had discovered *The Seven Storey Mountain* in 1952 while hitch-hiking across the country and it had influenced his decision to abandon his anthropology studies and turn to a life of Zen meditation.

Of all the Beats, Jack Kerouac was the one most sympathetic to the traditional forms of Roman Catholicism. He had been raised by a devout French-Canadian Catholic mother who made sure that he attended mass regularly and as Kerouac grew older he returned closer and closer to his Catholic roots. In 1949, shortly after *The Seven Storey Mountain* was published, Jack read it with fervor and enthusiastically recommended it to his friend Ginsberg, who finally read it in 1954. Ginsberg was a friend of both Kerouac and Lax, and said that they "had a lot of correspondence and sent poems back and forth to each other and talked about Merton and I guess Kerouac read *The Seven Storey Mountain* which was about Columbia, and maybe read other books later on that were sent him by Merton or by Lax."

As he grew older, Kerouac took up drawing and painting and produced hundreds of pictures on religious themes as his writings became even more infused with the spiritual desire he felt. In later interviews, he would depart from his earlier declaration that "beat" meant beaten down and increasingly defined the word "beat" to mean beatific. He wrote that "I'm actually not a Beat but a strange solitary crazy Catholic mystic." It isn't difficult to imagine that if he had to do it over again, Kerouac might have chosen the same path that Merton took.

Even the outspoken and uninhibited poet Allen Ginsberg had a lot in common with Merton. Before Allen read *The Seven Storey Mountain*, he had already read some of Merton's poetry in the earliest New Directions books and he had found them "wild and suggestive." In a letter from 1948 written to his college friend Paul Bertram complaining about critics like L.E. Sissman,[2] Ginsberg said "[I] suggest you read, for instance – the first few verses ("Weep like wax") in Merton's book. Merton wrote his book (and the little lyric that I think is fine that was quoted unfavorably) against the hard hearted people like L.E. Sissman, and wrote it out of a real agony and a retirement from a sinful world. Sissman doesn't even know what sin means, to judge from his prose."

For his part, Merton did not go so far as to say he loved Ginsberg's poetry, but he did feel it was important. A few years later, he would write to his friend, Ludovico Silva:

> Perhaps one of the few American U.S. poets that has something to say for everybody is [Allen] Ginsberg. Do you know him? ... When I read Ginsberg I do not feel at home with him or like him as I like [César] Vallejo or Nicanor Parra, but it is a curious experience of recognizing an authentic interpretation of a society in which I live and from which I am in many ways alien. Ginsberg speaks a language I know because I hear it every day, and yet he is remote also. He talks about a country of which I happen to be a citizen, and yet it is not 'mine.' As a matter of fact, in many ways I have no country at all. The country in which I live is incomprehensible. I think all the clichés about it are crazy, but I do not want to invent others. I do not know whether it is all headed for ruin, or what. A North American poet has to say something of this, and I think the merit of Ginsberg is that he is authentic and does not judge. On the other hand I think it is a pity that it all has to be done with drugs...

After having experienced an early epiphany, Allen went on to spend the rest of his life searching for a spiritual path,

---

[2] L.E. Sissman (1928-1976) was known as the class poet at Harvard in the 1940s.

another similarity between the Beats and Merton. One day in 1948, Allen experienced the presence of William Blake, the same 18th century visionary poet who had been instrumental in Merton's conversion to Catholicism. Ginsberg heard Blake reciting poetry and "heard his voice commanding and prophesying to me from eternity, felt my soul open completely wide all its doors and windows and the cosmos flowed thru me, and experienced a state of altered apparently total consciousness so fantastic and science-fictional I even got scared later, at having stumbled on a secret door in the universe all alone." His auditory visitation led to a revelation of all the mysteries of the cosmos that lasted for a few minutes. It was an event that dramatically changed his life and he spent more than a decade trying to duplicate that visionary experience, sometimes through experimentation with a wide variety of drugs.

Merton underwent a similar type of visionary experience on a street corner in Louisville, Kentucky. On March 18, 1958, as he was walking through the downtown shopping district, he stopped at the corner of Walnut and Fourth Streets, where he was "overwhelmed with the realization that I loved all these people, that they were mine and I theirs, that we could not be alien to one another even though we were total strangers..." "If only everybody could realize this! But it cannot be explained." They were all "walking around shining like the sun," he later wrote. He saw that everyone was sacred, just as Ginsberg had declared that everyone was "holy." The two poets had much more in common than either one would care to believe. Of course, Ginsberg's visions led him to a short stint in a mental hospital, while Merton was able to return to the monastic life and ponder the incident in quiet isolation.

Gregory Corso also had his own visionary experience one day on the Greek island of Hydra. After describing his vision to J Laughlin, J wrote back to him, thanking him for the letter and mentioning that he had had a vision himself one day while skiing in the mountains. "It was really quite shattering", he wrote, continuing:

But these are experiences, I guess, which you can't invoke. At least I can't. I often talk about them with my friend Tom Merton down at the monastery. He has read all the Catholic mystics closely, and written about them, and in his own life of contemplation he attempts to get himself to that state, though I'm not certain that he ever quite makes it, because, for all of being locked up in the monastery, he is terribly interested in what is going on in the world, in people, and their doings. I think you might be interested in what Tom has been writing recently.

In addition to sending Merton new poetry from the outside world, J Laughlin also kept Ferlinghetti informed about Merton's poetry, which led to his sending Lawrence a copy of "Original Child Bomb" in the spring of 1961. Laughlin wrote explaining:

> What sets the poem apart is the new verbal tone, a mixture of satire and irony, fused into black humor, and a structure of depersonalization ... in which the speaker is much withdrawn from the content of the poem. It displays a departure from Tom's earlier religious poetry not only in content but in form. It is detached and documentary in style, but the effect is powerful. He took the title from the Japanese name for the atom bomb, since it was to be the first of its kind.

In his book *Thomas Merton and the Monastic Vision*, Lawrence Cunningham wrote that "The poem consisted of a series of excerpts from news accounts, articles, pilot diaries, news reports, etc. describing the dropping of the atomic bomb in the waning days of World War II. Reminiscent of the style popularized by the American novelist John Dos Passos in the thirties, Merton's desire was to highlight the horrors of manmade weapons of total destruction by a dispassionate account of the facts." Merton's poem represented a new direction that he was taking in his poetry. Aside from the strength of the poem, it struck a personal chord with Ferlinghetti too. Just a few weeks after the second atomic bomb was dropped on Nagasaki, Lawrence, as a young naval officer still on duty, toured the destruction and devastation of the city. He later said that the sights he witnessed that day instantly turned him into a pacifist.

Cover of the New Directions edition of Original Child Bomb, 1971.

ORIGINAL CHILD BOMB

POINTS FOR MEDITATION TO BE SCRATCHED ON THE WALLS OF A CAVE

1: In the year 1945 an Original Child was born. The name Original Child was given to it by the Japanese people, who recognized that it was the first of its kind.

2: On April 12th, 1945, Mr. Harry Truman became the President of the United States, which was then fighting the second world war. Mr. Truman was a vice president who became president by accident when his predecessor died of a cerebral hemorrhage. He did not know as much about the war as the president before him did. He knew a lot less about the war than many people did.

About one hour after Mr. Truman became president, his aides told him about a new bomb which was being developed by atomic scientists. They called it the "atomic bomb". They said scientists had been working on it for six years and that it had so far cost two billion dollars. They added that its power was equal to that of twenty thousand tons of TNT. A single bomb could destroy a city. One of those present added, in a reverent tone, that the new explosive might eventually destroy the whole world.

But Admiral Leahy[3] told the president the bomb would never work.

---

[3] Admiral Leahy. William D. Leahy (1875-1959) was the highest ranking member of the military and chairman of the Joint Chiefs of Staff under Roosevelt and Truman.

3: President Truman formed a committee of men to tell him if this bomb would work, and if so, what he should do with it. Some members of this committee felt that the bomb would jeopardize the future of civilization. They were against its use. Others wanted it to be used in demonstration on a forest of cryptomeria trees, but not against a civil or military target. Many atomic scientists warned that the use of atomic power in war would be difficult and even impossible to control. The danger would be very great. Finally, there were others who believed that if the bomb were used just once or twice, on one or two Japanese cities, there would be no more war. They believed the new bomb would produce eternal peace.

4: In June 1945 the Japanese government was taking steps to negotiate for peace. On one hand the Japanese ambassador tried to interest the Russian government in acting as a go-between with the United States. On the other hand, an unofficial approach was made secretly through Mr. Allen Dulles[4] in Switzerland. The Russians said they were not interested and that they would not negotiate. Nothing was done about the other proposal which was not official. The Japanese High Command was not in favor of asking for peace, but wanted to continue the war, even if the Japanese mainland were invaded. The generals believed that the war should continue until everybody was dead. The Japanese generals were professional soldiers.

5: In the same month of June, the President's committee decided that the new bomb should be dropped on a Japanese city. This would be a demonstration of the bomb on a civil and military target. As "demonstration" it would be a kind of a "show". "Civilians" all over the world love a good "show". The "destructive" aspect of the bomb would be "military".

---

[4] Allen Dulles (1893-1969) during the war headed the O.S.S. in Switzerland and later became the first director of the CIA.

6: The same committee also asked if America's friendly ally, the Soviet Union, should be informed of the atomic bomb. Someone suggested that this information would make the Soviet Union even more friendly than it was already. But all finally agreed that the Soviet Union was now friendly enough.

7: There was discussion about which city should be selected as the first target. Some wanted it to be Kyoto, an ancient capital of Japan and a center of the Buddhist religion. Others said no, this would cause bitterness. As a result of a chance conversation, Mr. Stimson[5], the Secretary of War, had recently read up on the history and beauties of Kyoto. He insisted that this city should be left untouched. Some wanted Tokyo to be the first target, but others argued that Tokyo had already been practically destroyed by fire raids and could no longer be considered a "target." So it was decided Hiroshima was the most opportune target, as it had not yet been bombed at all. Lucky Hiroshima! What others had experienced over a period of four years would happen to Hiroshima in a single day! Much time would be saved, and "time is money!"

8: When they bombed Hiroshima they would put the following out of business: The Ube Nitrogen Fertilizer Company; the Ube Soda Company; the Nippon Motor Oil Company; the Sumitoma Chemical Company; the Sumitoma Aluminum Company; and most of the inhabitants.

9: At this time some atomic scientists protested again, warning that the use of the bomb in war would tend to make the United States unpopular. But the President's committee was by now fully convinced that the bomb had to be used. Its use would arouse the attention of the Japanese military class and give them food for thought.

---

[5] Henry Stimson (1867-1950) was the U.S. Secretary of War during WWII.

10: Admiral Leahy renewed his declaration that the bomb would not explode.

11: On the 4th of July, when the United States in displays of fireworks celebrates its independence from British rule, the British and Americans agreed together that the bomb ought to be used against Japan.

12: On July 7th the Emperor of Japan pleaded with the Soviet Government to act as mediator for peace between Japan and the Allies. Molotov[6] said the question would be "studied." In order to facilitate this "study" Soviet troops in Siberia prepared to attack the Japanese. The Allies had, in any case, been urging Russia to join the war against Japan. However, now that the atomic bomb was nearly ready, some thought it would be better if the Russians took a rest.

13: The time was coming for the new bomb to be tested, in the New Mexico desert. A name was chosen to designate this secret operation. It was called "Trinity".

14: At 5:30 A.M. on July 16th, 1945 a plutonium bomb was successfully exploded in the desert at Almagordo, New Mexico. It was suspended from a hundred foot steel tower which evaporated. There was a fireball a mile wide. The great flash could be seen for a radius of 250 miles. A blind woman miles away said she perceived light. There was a cloud of smoke 40,000 feet high. It was shaped like a toadstool.

15: Many who saw the experiment expressed their satisfaction in religious terms. A semi-official report even quoted a religious book – The New Testament, "Lord, I believe, help thou my unbelief." There was an atmosphere of devotion. It was a great act of faith. They believed the explosion was exceptionally powerful.

---

[6] Vyacheslav Molotov (1890-1986) was the Russian Minister of Foreign Affairs.

16: Admiral Leahy, still a "doubting Thomas," said that the bomb would not explode when dropped from a plane over a city. Others may have had "faith," but he had his own variety of "hope".

17: On July 21st a full written report of the explosion reached President Truman at Potsdam. The report was documented by pictures. President Truman read the report and looked at the pictures before starting out for the conference. When he left his mood was jaunty and his step was light.

18: That afternoon Mr. Stimson called on Mr. Churchill, and laid before him a sheet of paper bearing a code message about the successful test. The message read "Babies satisfactorily born." Mr. Churchill was quick to realize that there was more in this than met the eye. Mr. Stimson satisfied his legitimate curiosity.

19: On this same day sixty atomic scientists who knew of the test signed a petition that the bomb should not be used against Japan without a convincing warning and an opportunity to surrender.

At this time the U.S.S. Indianapolis, which had left San Francisco on the 18th, was sailing toward the island of Tinian, with some U 235 in a lead bucket. The fissionable material was about the size of a softball, but there was enough for one atomic bomb. Instructions were that if the ship sank, the Uranium was to be saved first, before any life. The mechanism of the bomb was on board the U.S.S. Indianapolis, but it was not yet assembled.

20: On July 26th the Potsdam declaration was issued. An ultimatum was given to Japan: "Surrender unconditionally or be destroyed." Nothing was said about the new bomb. But pamphlets dropped all over Japan threatened "an enormous air bombardment" if the army would not surrender. On July

26th the U.S.S. Indianapolis arrived at Tinian and the bomb was delivered.

21: On July 28th, since the Japanese High Command wished to continue the war, the ultimatum was rejected. A censored version of the ultimatum appeared in the Japanese press with the comment that it was "an attempt to drive a wedge between the military and the Japanese people." But the Emperor continued to hope that the Russians, after "studying" his proposal, would help to negotiate a peace. On July 30th Mr. Stimson revised a draft of the announcement that was to be made after the bomb was dropped on the Japanese target. The statement was much better than the original draft.

22: On August 1st the bomb was assembled in an air-conditioned hut on Tinian. Those who handled the bomb referred to it as "Little Boy." Their care for the Original Child was devoted and tender.

23: On August 2nd President Truman was the guest of His Majesty King George VI on board the H.M.S. Renown in Plymouth Harbor. The atomic bomb was praised. Admiral Leahy, who was present, declared that the bomb would not work. His Majesty George VI offered a small wager to the contrary.

24: On August 2nd a special message from the Japanese Foreign Minister was sent to the Japanese Ambassador in Moscow. "It is requested that further efforts be exerted… Since the loss of one day may result in a thousand years of regret, it is requested that you immediately have a talk with Molotov." But Molotov did not return from Potsdam until the day the bomb fell.

25: On August 4th the bombing crew on Tinian watched a movie of "Trinity" (the Almagordo Test). August 5th was a Sunday but there was little time for formal worship. They said a quick prayer that the war might end "very soon." On that day, Colonel Tibbetts, who was in command of the B-29 that was to drop the bomb, felt that his bomber ought to have a name. He baptized it Enola Gay, after his mother in Iowa. Col. Tibbetts was a well balanced man, and not sentimental. He did not have a nervous breakdown after the bombing, like some of the other members of his crew.

26: On Sunday afternoon "Little Boy" was brought out in procession and devoutly tucked away in the womb of Enola Gay. That evening few were able to sleep. They were as excited as little boys on Christmas Eve.

27: At 1:37 A.M. August 6th the weather scout plane took off. It was named the Straight Flush, in reference to the mechanical action of a water closet. There was a picture of one, to make this evident.

28: At the last minute before taking off Col. Tibbetts changed the secret radio call sign from "Visitor" to "Dimples." The bombing mission would be a kind of flying smile.

29: At 2:45 A.M. Enola Gay got off the ground with difficulty. Over Iwo Jima she met her escort, two more B-29's, one of which was called the Great Artiste. Together they proceeded to Japan.

30: At 6:40 they climbed to 31,000 feet, the bombing altitude. The sky was clear. It was a perfect morning.

31: At 8:09 they reached Hiroshima and started the bomb run. The city was full of sun. The fliers could see the green grass in the gardens. No fighters rose up to meet them. There was no flak. No one in the city bothered to take cover.

32: The bomb exploded within 100 feet of the aiming point. The fireball was 18,000 feet across. The temperature at the center of the fireball was 100,000,000 degrees. The people who were near the center became nothing. The whole city was blown to bits and the ruins all caught fire instantly everywhere, burning briskly. 70,000 people were killed right away or died within a few hours. Those who did not die at once suffered great pain. Few of them were soldiers.

33: The men in the plane perceived that the raid had been successful, but they thought of the people in the city and they were not perfectly happy. Some felt they had done wrong. But in any case they had obeyed orders. "It was war."

34: Over the radio went the code message that the bomb had been successful: "Visible effects greater than Trinity... Proceeding to Papacy." Papacy was the code name for Tinian.

35: It took a little while for the rest of Japan to find out what had happened to Hiroshima. Papers were forbidden to publish any news of the new bomb. A four line item said that Hiroshima had been hit by incendiary bombs and added: "It seems that some damage was caused to the city and its vicinity."

36: Then the military governor of the Prefecture of Hiroshima issued a proclamation full of martial spirit. To all the people without hands, without feet, with their faces falling off, with their intestines hanging out, with their whole bodies full of radiation, he declared: "We must not rest a single day in our war effort... We must bear in mind that the annihilation of the stubborn enemy is our road to revenge." He was a professional soldier.

37: On August 8th Molotov finally summoned the Japanese Ambassador. At last neutral Russia would give an answer to the Emperor's inquiry. Molotov said coldly that the Soviet Union was declaring war on Japan.

38: On August 9th another bomb was dropped on Nagasaki, though Hiroshima was still burning. On August 11th the Emperor overruled his high command and accepted the peace terms dictated at Potsdam. Yet for three days discussion continued, until August 14th the surrender was made public and final.

39: Even then the Soviet troops thought they ought to fight in Manchuria "just a little longer." They felt that even though they could not, at this time, be of help in Japan, it would be worth while if they displayed their good will in Manchuria, or even in Korea.

40: As to the Original Child that was now born, President Truman summed up the philosophy of the situation in a few words, "We found the bomb" he said "and we used it."

41: Since that summer many other bombs have been "found." What is going to happen? At the time of writing, after a season of brisk speculation, men seem to be fatigued by the whole question.

As it so happened, it was exactly the type of poem that Ferlinghetti was looking for to include in a new publication he had in mind. Two other San Francisco poets, Michael McClure and David Meltzer, had been meeting with Lawrence in hopes of publishing a new magazine that would address the major issues of 1961. Their prospectus stated: "We hope we have here an open place where normally apolitical men may speak uncensored upon any subject they feel most hotly & coolly about in a world which politics has made. We are not interested in protecting beings from themselves, we cannot help the deaths people give themselves, we are more concerned with the lives they do not allow themselves to live and the deaths other people would give us, both of the body & spirit." It seemed as if "Original Child Bomb" was written with that statement in mind.

In early May 1961, Lawrence wrote to the poet Gregory Corso to ask him to submit something for their first issue. He said he wanted "a lot of non-political writers and thinkers and poets and artists to make a statement on the state of the world at that time."

May 2, 1961
Cher Gregoire:
    Have you heard about [our] new *Journal For The Protection Of All Beings* which McClure, Meltzer & I are going to put out in June – Please can you send us prose blast on any subject like Peace, Disarmament, Non-violent action, Narcotics laws, Chessman,[7] Cuba, Algeria, etc etc.? Just a page or two will do.
    Luv-
    Lorenzo

---

[7] Caryl Chessman (1921-1960). Chessman was convicted and executed for a series of crimes he committed in Los Angeles a decade earlier. While awaiting execution, he wrote 4 books and became the focus of those who opposed the death penalty.

Two days later Ferlinghetti wrote to Ginsberg reminding him to send something for their new magazine. Ginsberg was in Europe with Peter Orlovsky and Gregory Corso and they were now all on their way to visit William S. Burroughs in Morocco. Since Allen was often in contact with local writers when he traveled, Lawrence asked him to try to get writings from some of the notable Europeans. He wrote, assuming a fake, hip dialogue that he sometimes used at the time.

May 4, 1961
Cher Allen:

McClure wrote you bout our new greata *Revolutionary Journal For The Protection Of All Beings* – Hope you can really catch some of those big dogs over there like Sartre and Beckett (especially Beckett) and Genet and Celine and get page or two from each – prose blasts or capsule essays on whatever subject they're heated up about at the moment – revelations – McClure covered all this to you – It will be large-size newsprint journal, format like *Hasty Papers* [8] only not THAT large – We'll print a lot and get it all over country. So send something in prose yourself. It's going to be terrific, if all the writers we wrote come thru....

Leroi [Jones] is now bugged with me since, after big exchange of telegrams, I refused to sign his declaration by poets & artists, sponsored by Casa de las Americas in Havana and also signed by many South American writers. I wouldn't sign because no one in US government is going to be persuaded to change US policy toward Cuba (or to change its plans for future invasions) by our declaring our solidarity with foreign writers sponsored by Cuban organization. Who does he think such a

---

[8] *Hasty Papers* was a one-issue magazine put out by Alfred Leslie.

Declaration would influence in this country? It would only give bait to witchhunters wanting to hang any of us who oppose US gov policy in Cuba and would compromise independent position of dissent. I wonder if Mailer signed this. Did you & Gregory? No one here (in SF) did, far as I know.... I bet Jack [Kerouac] didn't (He got his own Revolution out dere).... I figure we're not playing games anymore, daddy ....

Let me hear
Cookoo
Lorenzo

At the end of May, Lawrence received a letter from Ginsberg saying that he had nothing to send to him for his new *Journal*. He suggested what he called a "spontaneous manifesto on Cuba" that he had written with Corso and Orlovsky. It had just been published in a European newspaper after the failed Bay of Pigs Invasion that April. As for other European writers, Allen said "Am not now in touch with anyone of the big dogs so can't collect material." Ferlinghetti knew it was essential to include Ginsberg and Corso in the *Journal* and so he persisted. He had written to a great many people for contributions and had received very few answers. "We were hoping for political or trans-political statements from many people like Merton [but] many never answered," Lawrence said.

5 June 61
Dear Allen ....

Could we have first part of "Fall of America" for our new journal? Maybe the first, 3 or 4 pages of it?? If none of that, we cud use your "When the Mode of the Music Changes the Walls of the City Shake", from *Second Coming*. How 'bout that? We now have Norman Mailer letter to Castro & JFK, Gary

Snyder's Buddhist anarchism, [Robert] Duncan's gnosticism (not sure of title), [my] "Picturesque Haiti," McClure's "Revolt" (from his essay in *Meat Science*) and are also thinking of printing Artaud's "To Have Finished With Judgement Of God" in Guy Wernham translation. Would you know anything about the "rights" to this last? I'm still trying to get copy of [the] LaGuardia Report[9] – no luck yet – still trying to get hold of Dr. Bowman[10].... Can you send us that spontaneous manifesto on Cuba published in Paris? We never got copy. Also never got Gregory's [Corso] *American Express*. Ask him cd we excerpt from it for *Journal?*

OK – Yss – Cookoo –

Lorenzo

Having by now received a copy of Merton's "Original Child Bomb" via Laughlin, Ferlinghetti wrote a much more formal letter to Merton asking permission to publish the poem. In his role as editor and publisher, he also made a few editorial suggestions to improve the poem and correct some things he felt were not accurate.

June 30, 1961

Dear Merton:

J. Laughlin has very kindly let me read your Original Child Bomb, and we would like to use it in our new *Journal for the Protection of All Beings*, the first issue having articles on capital punishment, disarmament, non-violent action,

---

[9] The LaGuardia Report was issued in 1944 and was the first detailed study of the use of marijuana.

[10] Karl M. Bowman (1888-1973) was a well-known psychiatrist at Langley-Porter Hospital in San Francisco who was suggested by Ginsberg as a possible source for a copy of the LaGuardia Report.

sumptuary laws, hunger. J says we could use it before he makes a pamphlet[11] of it, without conflicting with plans, if OK with you.

The end of it bothers me, and I am wondering if you ever read Lapp's "Brighter Than a Thousand Suns"[12] or an article by Norman Cousins and Admiral Finletter which appeared in a book on American foreign policy edited by William A. Williams.[?][13] Both of these books made the following point, among others: The facts are that it was agreed at Yalta that Russia would enter the Japanese war at a certain date. Then when Roosevelt died and Truman took over, the atom bomb still was not revealed to the Russians, and the date of its dropping was advanced so that it would precede Russian entry into the War, since it then appeared we could end the War without the Russians and thus avoid their being in on the spoils. Thus, considering these circumstances (revealed in Truman's memoirs and by Finletter), to say sarcastically that Russia "bravely" entered the War after the Bomb was dropped is to leave yourself open to some sharp rebuttals. This is also true of your last sentence about Russia having won the War in three days. I'm afraid this will be taken as a

---

[11] In 1962, New Directions published *Original Child Bomb* in an edition of 8,000 copies.

[12] Actually, Robert Jungk wrote *Brighter Than a Thousand Suns* (Harcourt, Brace and Company, 1956). Ralph Lapp was an American Manhattan Project physicist whose writing echoed the same anti-atomic bomb sentiments. Lapp was the first person to sign Leo Szliard's petition against the dropping of the atomic bomb on Japan.

[13] Williams, William Appleman. *The Tragedy of American Diplomacy.* Cleveland: World Publishing Co., 1959. Norman Cousins and Thomas K. Finletter's article was written in 1946 and titled "A Beginning for Sanity." Finletter was never an admiral but served as the Secretary of the Air Force from 1950-53. In 1961, he was appointed Ambassador to NATO, which is perhaps the title Ferlinghetti mistook as Admiral.

rather coy ending, especially since the rest of the piece is so powerful (and accurate). I hope you will not be annoyed by my brashness in making these comments and suggestions, but I do feel strongly that the present ending more or less weakens all that has preceded it, and perhaps you will be willing to write a stronger ending for it. (You might, for instance, carry the religious symbolism of the bomb (and its project names) to a final point????)

In any case, I'll wait to hear from you, before returning your ms. to J.... By the way, he asked me to send you Ginsberg's *Kaddish*, and we have just mailed it to you separately, by book post.....

With very best wishes,
Lawrence Ferlinghetti

PS I do not necessarily have a pro-Russian ending in mind at all. But the whole article up to the end is seemingly against the Bomb. Then at the end you turn the whole thing against Russia, as if Russia were responsible for dropping it (or for its development)...! It was our bomb, we dropped it, so why blame Russians for not participating in what was kept secret from them? etc etc. All this is illogical, *n'est-ce pas*?

The *Journal For The Protection Of All Beings* was developing slowly, but by this time Ferlinghetti still hadn't received anything from Corso in Morocco. Lawrence, along with Joanna and Michael McClure, collaborated to write the following letter, very much in the idiom of the times. They used the fact that Merton had given them something to further entice Corso into sending a poem instead of using an entire play of his as he had suggested. Michael began by praising the play, but said it wouldn't work in the *Journal* format they had in mind.

[Dear Gregory]
   POEMS O.K.
Gregory by the hair on your bloody fuck
if that is not a nice beginning for a play, oh
blessed drama to be finished somewhere... but
is not drama to be enacted and heard? We are
listening and waiting for each and everyone to
make a speech that can be played out in type for
the guy who will listen dropping in off the street
into City Lights or the book stores of Indiana
right this minute or some coming instant
regarding these instantaneous and immediate
happenings of life and death – believing that
the faith of these persons has been misplaced
by the poisons of newspaper – and do not hide
behind the defenses of Shelley in his defenses
of poetry – and you never have, and are not
accused ... and surely you are remembering
his dictum that the names and persons of the
contemporary are immediately controvertible to
poetry... but let us have an instant cry and vision
of this immediatated moment and second!

   To eat the rose is not the same as being one.
Speak of the root of the earth of that green
energy; a force of rose-energy; the direct giving.
Get the old man out & let the child come forth!

   Come down from ether space and tell direct
about saint Moroccan garbage deity walking
down the street of Tangier eating tangerine and
blowing green smoke of pure humanity, give us
lowdown of Algerian bone-grindings trying to
tear loose from France, and what are they doing
in Morocco about neutron bombs about to
blow away their kif[14] killing everybody without
destroying even one window of building or
puncturing a tire, and the main thing being to
say it in such a non in-group way that, as said

---

[14] kif, a slang term for cannabis.

above, every cube cat in Hastings Indiana will be able to get it....Burrows [William Burroughs] sit and make picky pick at nose thinking of little boy make fucky fuck but now is interesting know why he want make that and straighten sad Kat thinking of same somewhere while much important Genet cat him say can no talk regarding bare facts of life that destroy self-statutes of literature as yet unbuilt in civic squares of Australasia. A.G. [Ginsberg] talk in void of dreams as he talk lovely in life somewhere regarding ancient recently dead while Janey McClure[15] smallest of the voices of contemporary physiology having quietly said 'goom goom' at about the same time as Lion is now saying things of vaster new import as always constantly changing. Constant roar to prepare open ear for one titanic silence if it be immense food now gone all stale & FOR GOD'S SAKE shit it out & lay the earth wet? immediate instant giving shit!

This is written in the very style which we do not want to publish in journal! We want extremely lucid essay-blasts laying out subjects such as Gary Snyder's "Buddhist Anarchism", Meltzer's "Cerebral Hemorrhage" (rundown on boxers who died in the ring this year), Thomas Merton's "Original Child Bomb" (factual description of dropping of Hiroshima bomb, in strange religious light), etc, etc, (all these are to be in first issue)....

What's easy is getting hard to respond to. The bunched nerve tongue holds up no song; but clak click clunk repeat, not constant, merely easy: all muscle easy to twitch & hop on shoulders look over the stomach city cut open laid out for vulture & parade. Instant parade of

---

[15] Janey McClure is Joanna and Michael McClure's daughter.

one brass spirt.

Send "statements" (not plays or such!) and postage refunded!

Michael

Give out w/love, sing!

Jo Ann

For *Journal Protection* All Go Mad Sing Music Beings

Lorenzo

In the meantime, James Laughlin informed Ferlinghetti that it might create a problem for Merton if his superiors found out that he was to be published in a "beat" magazine. They might see it as guilt by association with a beatnik group who were little more than juvenile delinquents flocking to American cities in droves. Lawrence Lipton called them "holy barbarians" and they were not the right kind of people for good Catholics to be associating with. Although Ferlinghetti desperately wanted to include Merton's poem in the *Journal*, he hoped that it would not cause any trouble for Tom within the monastic community. Lawrence wrote back to him respectfully trying to alleviate any fears he might have.

4 July 1961

Dear Merton -

J Laughlin tells me you do not want to be identified with any group, thru the publication of your article, and I hasten to assure you that our new *Journal* is not being published by any particular group or grouping of writers, and that we have no political affiliation, being completely independent in every way. The only bond between the articles in our first issue is a humanitarian one... I hope this will allay your doubts! We are eager to use your Child Bomb.

Yours most faithfully

Lawrence F.

Behind the scenes, the "Original Child Bomb" had also been sent to Merton's old friend Robert Lax who was now eager to publish it in his own magazine, *Pax*. Merton felt that it might be better to withdraw the poem from Ferlinghetti's *Journal* and submit something else in its place. He decided that another poem he had recently written, "Chant To Be Used In Processions Around A Site With Furnaces," might be a better choice and so he sent a manuscript of that to Ferlinghetti. He warned that he would have to first submit that one to the Catholic censors, but he hoped that it might be an acceptable replacement.

The poem was also in Merton's new style, which he called an "anti-poem," similar to the anti-poems of Nicanor Parra. It was a poem that was stripped of the "superficial trimmings of poetry, it's poetic language," as it was later defined by Paul Pearson, the director of the Thomas Merton Center. This poem echoed the same basic anti-war values as his "Original Child Bomb." It evoked Auschwitz as told from the point of view of the death camp's commandant. "In truth this poem is composed almost in its entirety from the very words of the commanders of Auschwitz," Thomas wrote later. "It would be impossible to invent something more terrifying than the truth itself."

As Lawrence Cunningham described it: "The poem used factual data gleaned from books Merton read, but unlike Child Bomb this work does not speak in neutral 'journalistic' tones; the voice drips with irony and open sarcasm." If anything, the new poem was even more to Ferlinghetti's liking because irony and sarcasm were characteristic of his own poetry. At the time, Merton also proposed using a pseudonym instead of publishing it under his own name, which he thought might make it easier to by-pass the church censors.

CHANT TO BE USED IN PROCESSIONS AROUND A SITE WITH FURNACES

How we made them sleep and purified them

How we perfectly cleaned up the people and worked a big heater

I was the commander I made improvements and installed a guaranteed system taking account of human weakness I purified and I remained decent

How I commanded

I made cleaning appointments and then I made the travellers sleep and after that I made soap[16]

I was born into a Catholic family but as these people were not going to need a priest I did not become a priest I installed a perfectly good machine it gave satisfaction to many

When trains arrived the soiled passengers received appointments for fun in the bathroom they did not guess

---

[16] It was widely believed that the Nazis made soap out of the flesh of the Jews they had exterminated.

It was a very big bathroom for two thousand people
it awaited their arrival and they arrived safely

There would be an orchestra of merry widows not
all the time much art

If they arrived at all they would be given a greeting
card to send home taken care of with good jobs
wishing you would come to our joke

Another improvement I made was I built the
chambers for two thousand invitations at a time the
naked votaries were disinfected with Zyklon B[17]

Children of tender age were always invited by reason
of their youth they were unable to work they were
marked out for play

They were washed like the others and more than the
others

Very frequently women would hide their children in
the piles of clothing but of course when we came
to find them we would send the children into the
chamber to be bathed

How I often commanded and made improvements
and sealed the door on top there were flowers the
men came with crystals I guaranteed always the
crystal parlor

I guaranteed the chamber and it was sealed you
could see through portholes

They waited for the shower it was not hot water that
came through vents though efficient winds gave full
satisfaction portholes showed this

---

[17] Zyklon B was the poison used in the death chambers.

The satisfied all ran together to the doors awaiting arrival it was guaranteed they made ends meet

How I could tell by screaming that love came to a full stop I found the ones I had made clean after about a half hour

Jewish male inmates then worked up nice they had rubber boots in return for adequate food I could not guess their appetite

Those at the door were taken apart out of a fully stopped love by rubber male inmates strategic hair and teeth being used later for defense

Then the males took off all clean love rings and made away with happy gold

A big new firm promoted steel forks operating on a cylinder they got the contract and with faultless workmanship delivered very fast goods

How I commanded and made soap 12 lbs fat 10 quarts water 8 oz to a lb of caustic soda but it was hard to find any fat

"For transporting the customers we suggest using light carts on wheels a drawing is submitted"

"We acknowledge four steady furnaces and an emergency guarantee"

"I am a big new commander operating on a cylinder I elevate the purified materials boil for 2 to 3 hrs and then cool"

For putting them into a test fragrance I suggested an express elevator operated by the latest cylinder it was guaranteed

Their love was fully stopped by our perfected ovens but the love rings were salvaged

Thanks to the satisfaction of male inmates operating the heaters without need of compensation our guests were warmed

All the while I had obeyed perfectly

So I was hanged in a commanding position with a full view of the site plant and grounds

You smile at my career but you would do as I did if you knew yourself and dared

In my day we worked hard we saw what we did our self sacrifice was conscientious and complete our work was faultless and detailed

Do not think yourself better because you burn up friends and enemies with long-range missiles without ever seeing what you have done

28 July 61
Dear Merton ...

Thank you for the new poem and letter. That is a very strong poem, though I don't see what objection Catholic censors could have to it, except perhaps that reference to the speaker's having been born Catholic. Perhaps if you left that phrase out, the censors would agree more easily? (Is Eichmann really a Catholic?)

Both Laughlin and myself are worried about your using that pseudonym for this, unless the Church knows you use a pseudonym now and then – and approves. You mean you are allowed to publish whatever you want to publish as long as you don't use your right name? The thing is, as Laughlin pointed out to me, that various people outside the Church will know this poem is yours – especially if you have sent out more than one copy. So is this Kosher with the Katholic censors? We are just ignorant of this subject chez vous and would like to know if all's really OK to proceed with the publication.....

I am a (non-practicing) Catholic, myself (not a Protestant, in any case), and you might be surprised to hear I wrote you about ten years ago about some question of consecrated virginity in Hildebrand's "Marriage."[18] Got a note from a secretary in return...

Thank you for the words as to our *Journal*. It is surprising how very few novelists, poets, or other creative writers have responded with anything we could use. And I have been mulling over an essay to be called "The Bankruptcy Of The Creative In The United States". The world going to hell in a handbag and all these great artists sitting around scratching and doing

---

[18] *Marriage: The Mystery of Faithful Love* by Dietrich Von Hildebrand was published in 1942.

nothing about it...

Also: How come no clergymen, priests, nuns,
and monks march in our Peace Parades?... The
Crusades weren't Peace Parades were they?.....

Yours most true,

Lawrence F.

Couldn't you somehow "rush through"
approval of that poem so that you can use your
own name on it? It's important.

Ferlinghetti was wrong in thinking that the poem was
about Adolf Eichmann, who supervised the deportation of
Jews to concentration camps during WWII. Eichmann's name
was on everyone's lips because he had recently been captured
and was about to be executed in an Israeli prison on June
1, 1962. The poem was actually based on the career of the
Nazi Rudolf Höss [Hoess] who was the commandant of the
Auschwitz concentration camp. Many of the statements were
taken directly from his testimony at the Nuremberg trials. For
example, during the trial Höss made the despicable comment
that "very frequently women would hide their children under
the clothes, but of course when we found them we would
send the children in to be exterminated." In his poem, Merton
used this statement almost verbatim.

Ferlinghetti desperately needed Merton's contribution
for, as he stated, so many writers were reluctant to take a
stand on anything political. If Ferlinghetti's own poetry was
anything, it was political. "Chant" was the perfect addition to
the small number of submissions they had received so far,
and having Merton as a part of it would entice other writers
to contribute and wouldn't hurt sales either. His name would
also lend moral weight to the other writers who were not yet
being taken quite as seriously.

Aug. 2, 1961

Dear Lawrence:

Since you ask me to, I have sent the furnace poem to the censors of the Order.[19] However, here is the thing: if they object to it we can't print it at all, whereas if I had printed it over a pseudonym it would at least be printed and they might object afterwards if they knew who wrote it, which would be quite doubtful.

Here we are dealing not with diocesan censors who confine themselves to matters of faith and morals, and are to be taken seriously, but with censors of the Order who bother their heads about everything, because they have been given the task of judging whether or not a piece of work is <u>opportune</u>. That word opportune covers a lot of ground. First of all it is intended explicitly to discourage new writers from arising in the Order. Secondly it is concerned with how the work of an established writer may be imagined to effect the reputation of the Order. This extends to some very picayune things. I had a frightful time publishing two articles on [Boris] Pasternak because of the implication that I must have read a) his novel and b) newspapers and magazines, which all would be a cataclysmic blow to the prestige of the Order. Utterly unthinkable. The atomic bomb piece was objected to on roughly the same grounds, though was put more coyly: "this has been written about before by others". In a word these cats are obsessed with a certain image they have of themselves and they don't want anyone disturbing it. What they want me to do is to build up the Order to the skies and

---

[19] On Aug. 5, 1961, fr. M. Thomas Aquinas Porter reviewed the poem, then on Aug 19, 1961 fr M. Gabriel O'Connell reviewed it, and on Aug. 31, 1961 fr. M. Gabriel Sortais (Abbé Général in Rome) approved the use of the poem as it was submitted.

make it look as if nobody in it even had a body any more, let alone five senses and an awareness that the rest of the universe continued to exist. This to me seems somehow unconnected with the Christian concept of charity which seems to me to indicate that the Christian is somehow involved with the rest of mankind and that they all have common problems. War for instance, and peace, and concentration camps. I regret that I have not yet advanced to the stage where I can be exclusively concerned with birth control and pornography as the only two moral problems worthy of concern, along with the sixth commandment,[20] generally referred to as "sin" without further qualification.

But I do have a moral problem about that furnace piece. A very sensitive guy who has been living in Europe and knows people who were in the camps, including a Jewish girl who was deliberately run over by a tank outside the Warsaw ghetto and lost her legs, says the piece is too nasty and that people aren't thinking that way over there. In a word the question of violence arises in the poem itself. Certainly it is not pro Auschwitz, but the fact remains that it states all these things in a sardonic manner which is non-committal and callous (apparently). Also the aspect of it which bothers me is: to what extent can we point to what is hateful and say it ought to be hated, if by that we necessarily imply that there are, therefore, people to be hated and punished? This piece is by the way not about Eichmann, but about the commandant of Auschwitz, Hoess.

Some day when I have thought about it more I want to talk to you about effective protest as distinct from a simple display of sensitivity

---

[20] Thou shalt not kill.

and good will. I think we have to examine the question of genuine and deep spiritual non-cooperation, non-participation, and resistance. There is so very little in this country that what little there is has got to be good. If it is not good, if it is just a question of standing up and saying with sincerity, candor and youthful abandon "I am against", it has the following bad effects. a) It perpetuates an illusion of free thought and free discussion, which is actually very useful to those who have long since stifled all genuine freedom in this regard. b) It flatters the squares by giving them something they can contrast themselves with, to their own complacent advantage. I leave you to work out some of the other implications. Have you by any chance read the Old Testament prophets lately? They knew how to hit hard in the right places, and the chief reason was that they were not speaking for themselves.

You ask me about why certain persons are absent from peace parades: because they themselves did not organize the peace parade. This is the main reason. They don't join with any other organization in doing things. Why haven't they organized one of their own? Because they are too busy shouting about the need for destroying the enemy. Why are they so busy shouting....? Etc. All down the line. Ultimately they think in negative terms. They define themselves by standing back from the guy that is something else, and say "at any rate I am not him" and they start from there to arrive at who they are. This I think is why there are so many zombies around. They are just not someone else. Nor are they themselves. This goes for everybody in whatever group, whoever does this, ends up a zombie.

I am sorry about the letter you wrote ten

years ago. Of course I don't remember whether or not I even got it. Mail is subject to all sorts of ups and downs. Sometimes you get most of it, sometimes very little of it, and sometimes someone who has been getting through to you regularly suddenly becomes nacht and nabel. A lot of the stuff sent to me is answered by a secretary in the Abbot's office, or handed to some other department. If you have since found yourself getting a lot of cheese advertising and come ons for donations to the monks, then your letter got into the office of one of the Fathers who is in charge of a big long mailing list.

Talking about mailing lists: could you send me some of your catalogues? I mean of paperbacks of all kinds that I could get from City Lights Bks?

Look, I don't give you the gotta go to confession right away routine. What is vitally important is that you should be a Christian and as faithful to the truth as you can get. This may mean anything but resembling some of the pious faithful. But I don't have to tell you, because you know, that there is only one thing that is of any importance in your life. Call it fidelity to conscience, or to the inner voice, or to the Holy Spirit: but it involves a lot of struggle and no supineness and you probably won't get much encouragement from anybody. There is a dimension of Catholicism, mostly French and German, which gives a little room for growth like this. But you have to find it as best you can. I can't necessarily tell you where to look, or how much of it you have found already. The start of it all is that none of us really have started to look. But the mercy of God, unknown and caricatured and blasphemed by some of the most reputable squares, is the central reality out

of which all the rest comes and into which all
the rest returns.

Have to stop. God bless you
Yours in Xt always,
Tom Merton

8 Aug 61
Dear Tom -

Thank you for the very interesting letter. I'm
afraid my query about using your pseudonym
has gotten us into a bind – since we sent your
"Furnace" to the printer the same day, leaving
the name blank. Now it seems there's a good
chance we won't be able to use it at all, if your
censors say so, and here we are almost ready to
run the issue. We will be able to hold up on it
until about August 17th, and I hope to have some
new word from you by then. It is already set in
type, and – since we are not rich – this makes a
difference. (I should have just gone ahead with
it, without worrying about the pseudonym) –
Your doubts about the threat of violence in the
text and about your German friend's reactions
– are not serious, I hope – Since I did not get
this same feeling from the text at all; and I hope
we'll be able to go ahead with it as-is (– even if
we print it under "Anonymous"?)

Hurriedly – yours
Lawrence

(I'll write you a decent letter next time.)
Sending you booklists separately, as requested.

Before he was able to receive an answer from Merton to
his letter, Ferlinghetti wrote another one suggesting that they
go back to using the "Original Child Bomb" poem instead

of the new "Chant." This set up a crossing of letters in the mail and a few more confused exchanges before it was all straightened out.

11 Aug 61
Dear Tom...

Here we are running around in our little circles in the brown world while you sit contemplating in your green landscape. I was disappointed about not being able to publish your "Furnace" now, but have just written Lax to ask him when *Pax* with "Child Bomb" in it is coming out. We have put off our first issue of *Journal* until mid-Sept, and maybe we can still use "Child Bomb" in it, since you said in your former letter that we could use it after *Pax*, as long as it did not also conflict with Laughlin's plans for it as a book. J says it is OK with him, so maybe Lax will also agree, since the audience reached by *Pax* and our *Journal* are not at all the same, and we are also in two different parts of the country. I left it up to Lax and hope to hear from him by return airmail. In the meantime, if you have changed the ending of the "Child Bomb" text, could you airmail me the final version? J is out of town at the moment, so I can't find out if he has the new version right away.

I'm sorry to bother you with all this rushing around, and I would not do it if we here did not feel "Child Bomb" so important. (We are liable all to be floating around in small irradiated pieces before we get anything printed, if we don't hurry!)

Pax, and thank you for your patience,

Lawrence

Robert Lax eventually published the "Original Child" poem later in the year without any changes made to the ending. It included illustrations by Emil Antonucci another friend of Merton's. Then New Directions published a separate version in December that reached a wider audience, but by that time Ferlinghetti had decided not to continue as the main editor of the *Journal.* The following letter, however, was in response to Lawrence's letter of Aug. 8, not the more recent Aug. 11 idea.

ABBEY OF GETHSEMANI
TRAPPIST, KENTUCKY

Aug. 12, 1961

Dear Lawrence:

Your letter requires a quick answer. Of course print the poem if it is set up. There is no question about that since I said you could do it if there was no name, or no right name.

But now: about the name. Here is what has happened so far. Of course nothing has come from the censor. But I sent a copy of the poem to Dorothy Day, just for her. And she passed it on to the boys at the Catholic Worker and now they, as far as I know, are printing or have printed it. Also without benefit of censorship, permission from me, and a few minor details like that. They did write, but it was already an accomplished fact, or so it appeared from the letter.

Since they have to all appearances printed the thing over my name, there is no further reason why you should not do so. The fat is in the fire, so you might as well go ahead and I will take responsibility with my Superiors for whatever follows. It is an accident and that is that. They may not be too happy about it, and it may make them clamp down on anything of this type in the future. But what can anyone do about it now? So go ahead.

I am glad at any rate that the magazine is coming right along and look forward to seeing it soon.

What have you decided to do about the Atomic Bomb piece? I have rewritten it, but don't know whether to send a copy to J out there or not. Nor do I know what has been decided by him and Lax and Antonucci. Perhaps I had better wait until Lax prints it and then let you print from his copy, if you want it.

More later. God bless you always.

In Christ

Tom.

Reproduction of letter from Merton to Ferlinghetti, 1961.

Aug. 12, 1961
Dear Lawrence:

Your letter requires a quick answer. Of course print the poem ["Chant"] if it is set up. There is no question about that since I said you could do it if there was no name, or no right name.

But now: about the name. Here is what has happened so far. Of course nothing has come from the censor. But I sent a copy of the poem to Dorothy Day,[21] just for her. And she passed it on to the boys at the *Catholic Worker* and now they, as far as I know, are printing or have printed it.[22] Also without benefit of censorship, permission from me, and a few minor details like that. They did write, but it was already an accomplished fact, or so it appeared from the letter.

Since they have, to all appearances printed the thing over my name, there is no further reason why you should not do so. The fat is in the fire, so you might as well go ahead and I will take responsibility with my Superiors for whatever follows. It is an accident and that is that. They may not be too happy about it, and it may make them clamp down on anything of this type in the future. But what can anyone do about it now? So go ahead.

I am glad at any rate that the magazine is coming right along and look forward to seeing it soon.

What have you decided to do about the Atomic Bomb piece? I have rewritten it, but don't know whether to send a copy to J out

---

[21] Dorothy Day (1897-1980) was the founder of *The Catholic Worker* newspaper and a leading social activist.

[22] "Chant To Be Used In Processions Around A Site With Furnaces" was printed in *The Catholic Worker*, vol. 28, no. 1 (July 1, 1961).

there or not. Nor do I know what has been decided by him and [Robert] Lax and [Emil] Antonucci.[23] Perhaps I had better wait until Lax prints it and then let you print from his copy, if you want it.

More later. God bless you always.

In Christ

Tom

How about that other poem?

Tuesday Aug 15

Dear Tom -

Your letter just arrived saying we could use your name and your "Chant (Furnace)" – so many, many thanks for this. We will use your name instead of "Anonymous" since *Catholic Worker* already has.... As for the "Child Bomb" we will now definitely wait until after Lax publishes it – Sorry to have bothered you with that rush letter a couple of days ago – All is OK now....

Enclosed is the little poem you recently sent which doesn't fit our *Journal* at the moment, and I see no reason to hold it when you can get it published elsewhere easily.

Thank you again for the time and patience involved in all this.

Yours most true –

Lawrence

Aug. 15, 1961

Dear Lawrence:

Your letter came this morning together with

---

[23] Emil Antonucci (1929-2006). Artist and book illustrator who worked with Robert Lax on many projects. He is perhaps most famous for designing the logo for the famous New York restaurant, The Four Seasons.

one from the *Catholic Worker* which confirms that they have printed the Auschwitz piece ["Chant"]. Since that is the case you might as well go ahead and use it, there are no further reasons for not doing so. Print it over my name. I think it is better for you to use this in the first issue. Lax is not moving so fast with the Bomb piece, so it would be better to wait on that one.

I am sending a second copy of the Bomb piece, this time the full corrected version. I have not sent one to J. I presume he can print from what Lax puts out. They are arranging something between them.

There is peace in ourselves, since we are Sons of God: but the difficulty is in knowing this and facing it. The reason why we do not live in paradise is that it is difficult to be simple. This is our work, though. It is terribly important that we try to understand it, though we cannot really do that. And there are no easy explanations, or cliché answers to questions about it. The answers are all night.

Like being simple enough to love everybody. Nice, on paper. On this I made a sermon, and I send it. This is supposed to be printed maybe by Claude Fredericks[24] in Vermont, at least he is looking at it first. So much for the sermon. What I preach I don't necessarily do, but from that I hope I have learned to expect no less from other people. At least that.

With all affection in Christ

Tom

Bomb & sermon under separate cover. Nice combination.

---

[24] Claude Fredericks (1923-2013) was a poet, printer, and publisher of the Banyan Press. He taught at Bennington College for thirty years. Fredericks did not publish the sermon at that time.

[Aug. 21, 1961]
Dear Tom...

I have just had a meeting with the other
two editors of our *Journal*, and it seems I have
fouled up the proceedings of our printing of
your work in our *Journal*. The other two editors
(David Meltzer & Michael McClure) have
been going ahead on the assumption that your
"Furnace Chant" was to be in the first issue,
and – not only is it set in type, but the table of
contents is also at the printer, with the "Chant"
listed <u>without</u> your name and without your
pseudonym. The table of contents has also
been given to various publicity people – book
editors, etc – again without your name – We
have also already had printed a little brochure
with the Contents listed – All this since you
first freely offered the "Chant" to us. (I then
proceeded to mess things up on my own, not
really comprehending what it would mean if
you applied to the censors to use the piece with
your name.) In any case, since we already have
over 500 advance orders from bookstores and
individuals for the first issue, based upon the
Table of Contents, the editors feel we have no
<u>honorable</u> alternative but to at least print your
"Chant" under the name "anonymous" since
our whole publication would be fouled up if
it were pulled out – and a lot of subscribers
<u>deceived</u>. (The piece is also set at the beginning
of the *Journal*, and the page numbers would be
upset by any change at this point).

All three of us (editors) feel so strongly
about the "Chant" – I have read it and reread
it this weekend – it is a <u>great</u> poem – and it is
important that it be printed <u>now</u>, before things
are blown up – we have lots of things in the
first issue on the Bomb but nothing on this.
It is followed by a statement on the Bomb by

Bertrand Russell.[25] (If you get it cleared by the censors later, we can – if you want – then list your name or pseudonym as the author of it in the second issue.)

If I had been in contact with the other editors every day, this would not have happened, but we all get together only once a week – and in this case it was two weeks – and I am <u>very</u> sorry to have caused confusion on this – We have decided (over my own idea of waiting till September) to go ahead with the printing of the *Journal* this week – things in the world are changing <u>so fast</u> – So – please FORGIVE AND BEAR WITH US - - - -

Yours most sincerely and truly,
Lawrence

---

[25] Bertrand Russell (1872-1970) was one of Britain's most famous philosophers and a Nobel laureate.

JOURNAL FOR THE PROTECTION OF ALL BEINGS

NO. 1   SAN FRANCISCO   1961

CITY LIGHTS BOOKS
$1.50

Cover of *Journal*, 1961.

Finally by the end of September, the first edition of *The Journal For The Protection Of All Beings* was published and distributed widely. It appears that City Lights' printer was able to insert Merton's name before it went to press, but possibly copies of an earlier printing exist which are anonymous. None have been found, however, after an extensive search. Lawrence spent a lot of his time over the next few months on matters of distribution, trying to earn back the money he had to invest in the journal's publication. By the time the issue was off the press, Michael McClure was in New York City so Lawrence wrote to him, sending him copies and hoping that he could help increase sales. He also wanted him to collect money owed to them for copies already sold on the East Coast. He didn't have any positive reviews that he could send him yet, but he did comment on William Hogan's short review which appeared in the September 14 issue of the *San Francisco Chronicle* in which Hogan said:

> The old Beat influence is strong and shrill here, and the men still tend to write like boys. Yet this is a healthy minority report, chiefly by the Baudelaires and Rimbauds of our time (Ginsberg, Corso, Merton, Duncan, but also the late Albert Camus and the very, very late Percy B. Shelley and the not quite late Bertrand Russell among them). Boldly stated, boldly printed, it is an example of the artifact that keeps the North Beach culture forever young (or boyish).

Sept 20
Dear Mike ...
    Got yr card & letter, thanx, glad you like production of *JOURNAL*, cover, etc. Enclosed are the reviews from *San Francisco Chronicle* & *Examiner*... the usual hostility to the "Beat"; little did I suspect that Merton was one! (see Hogan review)..... fuck them, what do you have

to do, hit them on the head with a condom to make them believe in Love....? Alan Watts[26] called especially to say *Journal* looked beautiful & that he was <u>ashamed not to be in it</u>. I'm afraid this is something Kennety (Rexroth)[27] will never do, would never do.... I'm still waiting for him to answer our letters, calls, etc. Sent him review copy; I sent out about 50 review copies. Will try to get Don Allen[28] to review it for *EVERGREEN*.... Watch for ads (tiny ones) in *Village Voice*, *NY Times* (Oct 1st, in latter). Glad to hear good news of *Journal* at 8th St Bookship.... Some typos slipped thru despite all our proofing: this seems inevitable unless you have big staff: it don't matter now anyway.... We got newsstand distributor here and L.A., and hope DeBoer will take it for East... Anyhow, we have now sent out over 1500 copies and still going strong, Dick McB. [McBride][29] not caught up yet with it, him flooded with shipping woik, etc.... Could you git interviewed on KPFA's New York station, WBAI as editor of *JOURNAL*? Ask [Ted] Wilentz[30] how git in touch wid em? Whut do leroi [Jones] & irving rosenthal & marc schleifer think of it...? (Dave [Meltzer] says Ron Loewinbrow [sic: Loewinsohn] came in wid wifer & made snide remawks bout it). ... Yesh we sent you nine more copies surface mail. Let me know if you want more now..... Is there someone at Grove you could lay a copy on, for review? ..... Maybe you can find much

---

[26] Alan Watts (1915-1973) was an influential British philosopher who wrote many books on Eastern religions, especially Zen.

[27] Kenneth Rexroth (1905-1982) was a San Francisco poet and critic.

[28] Donald Allen (1912-2004) was an editor of contemporary poetry best known for his seminal collection *The New American Poetry 1945-1960*.

[29] Dick McBride (1928-2012) was a poet and an employee at City Lights.

[30] Ted Wilentz (1915-2001) owned the 8th Street Bookshop in New York City.

cheaper printer in NY: printing prices in East about 25% cheaper than here, SF the most high in cuntry.... I can't make next production scene, someone else will have to be production man & managing ed. of it, next issue: I was hung up on it all summer & didn't get any writing done except one 4-page Berlin poem all summer & am so far in hole to printer (*Journal* bill is $2900) we can't publish any new books for a long time....

Luv -

Lawrence

Later... Don [Allen] suggests that we get Irving Rosenthal to review *JOURNAL* in *Evergreen Review* & says he is in NY now and you can reach him thru Grove if you don't have his address. Lay copy on him? (enclosed is review slip).....

So you're digging NY now and living in the Village and that's fine for you & Joanne. I passed by that way, it seems now, a long time ago: the Metropolitan, Carnegie, The Whitney, Art Students League, Columbia, Lewisohn Stadium night concerts in hot summer, Washington Square concerts, woodwinds in the upper Seventies (I was a classical cat in them days), living on West 13th Street, Downing Street, East 26th St, Bedford, shacked up with Columbia girl lawyer now dead still beautiful.....

L

Sept 27 ...

Dear Mike ...

Got your last card & etc. Enclosed is letter from Marc Schleifer with address in Cuba: I have answered him and also sent copy of *JOURNAL* & sent his manuscred back to him (without making copy). Mebbe you cd also answer his accusations etc? .... We sent you 10 review copies surface mail 2 days ago. Give one to *Kulchur*, to *Yugen*, etc.... We sent out about 50 review copies, but mainly to newspaps and columnists, none to literary mags (which don't ordinarily review other reviews) so none of NY quarterlies such as *Partisan* got copies. Did cover *NY Times Book Review, Trib, NY Post* (Call the guy there who wrote the articles on the Beats last year – Al Aronowitz – I sent him *Journal*). I also sent copy to Ed Fancher at *Village Voice* .... Glad to hear you're going to get on WBAI .... Paperbook Gallery has sent us orders for *JOURNAL* but owes us hundreds of dollars for last year of City Lights Books & we keep writing them we can't send new orders until they pay up, but they just keep sending in new orders and no $ .... I just wrote its owner, Marty Geisler again about it – maybe you could call him and tell him personally why they are not getting *JOURNAL* from us. But DeBoer, Selected Outlets, 102 Beverly Road, Bloomfield, NJ, is supposed to start handling it soon for all NY, altho they've not let us know definitely yet.... Anyway, you can tell stores to ask DeBoer for it. It would help goose them along the road..... Your words with [Morton] Subotnick's musick played here at OPUS TOO this week, as you probably know, but I wasn't there – hope to go to next performance, whenever; it got good review by Frankenstein here.

So see you later like
Lawrence

Although copies of the *Journal For The Protection of All Beings* had been available for a few weeks, the official publication date was given as October 1, 1961. It was also in October that Merton began to make more public statements about the role of the Christian in the struggle for peace both at home and abroad. "The duty of the Christian in this crisis is to strive with all his power and intelligence, with his faith, hope in Christ, and love for God and man to do the one task which God has imposed on us in the world today. That task is to work for the total abolition of war," he wrote in the *Catholic Worker*. Earlier Merton had already written in *No Man Is an Island* that "when action and contemplation dwell together, filling our whole life because we are moved in all things by the Spirit of God, then we are spiritually mature," and his poetry became an extension of that maturity.

Merton wrote to Laughlin: "By now, as you know, a series of accidents has led to the publication of the Auschwitz poem both in the *Catholic Worker* and Ferlinghetti's *Journal*. And it is still not censored. Since I am in the clear I have no sorrows about it, though I may get into some trouble." In the same letter, he wrote about his general feelings:

> Personally, I am more and more concerned about the question of peace and war. I am appalled by the way everyone simply sits around and acts as though everything were normal. It seems to me that I have an enormous responsibility myself, since I am read by a lot of people and yet I don't know what to begin to say and then I am as though bound and gagged by the censors, who though not maliciously reactionary are just obtuse and slow. This feeling of frustration is terrible. Yet what can one say? If I go around shouting 'abolish war' it will be meaningless. Yet at least some one has to say that.

In late November, Ferlinghetti wrote a personal letter to Merton as a friend, apologizing for not being in touch with him over the past month or two. He continued to fear that Merton would be in trouble with his Superiors for contributing to a "beatnik" magazine. He also apologized that many of the poets hadn't wanted to commit themselves to anything that might have the appearance of being too political. Ten years later he would expand on those thoughts in his poem "Populist Manifesto," which begins with the lines:

> Poets, come out of your closets,
> Open your windows, open your doors,
> You have been holed-up too long
> in your closed worlds.

He went on to scold everyone for chanting while Rome burns. He believed it was almost too late to do anything about the major problems of mankind.

> The hour of oming is over,
> the time for keening come,
> time for keening & rejoicing
> over the coming end
> of industrial civilization
> which is bad for earth & Man.

22 Nov 1961

Dear Tom

I take the occasion of being in bed with a strained back to write you a ballpoint scrawl.... I am very sorry not to have sent you some note with our *Journal* when it came out and I wish to apologize for a typo I think was made in your poem as well as in the note about you in the back (New Directions listed as your "princi<u>ple</u>" publisher). Also I hope the *Journal* itself did not cause you too much embarrassment – You had no way of knowing what company you would be in when it was published – There are things in it I would not have published had I had full control of editorial matters – but – I would be interested in your reaction to it as a whole – The kind of publication I had in mind was not exactly what we ended up with. (For one thing, many poets just could not be made to <u>commit</u> themselves or take a stand on anything.)

I have read with much interest your dialog with [D.T.] Suzuki in ND #17[31] – The one point (and very basic it seems to be) upon which you and he could not make any real <u>rapprochement</u> is that of the <u>effectiveness</u> which you return to in rebuttal and insist upon, if I am not mistaken – of course I am not qualified to evaluate your arguments in this matter – but it seems to me that Suzuki's statement (on page 96) differentiating (1) the effective, personal and dualistic and (2) the non-effective, non-personal and non dualistic – is about the nub of the matter and cannot be talked away, no matter how much good will on either side. Perhaps another expression of

---

[31] The essay "Wisdom and Empty" appeared in *New Directions in Prose and Poetry*, no. 17 (1961).

Dear Tom I take the occasion of being in bed with a
strained back to write you a ballpoint scrawl.... I am
very sorry not to have sent you some note with our
JOURNAL when it came out + I wish to apologize for
a typo I think was made in ~~the~~ your poem as well as in the
note about you in the back (New Directions listed as your "principal
publisher"). Also I hope the JOURNAL itself did not cause
you too much embarassment — You had no way of knowing
what company you would be in when it was published —
There are things in it I would not have published had I had
full control of editorial matters — but — I would be interested
in your reaction to it as a whole — The kind of publication
I had in mind was not exactly what we ended up with
(For one thing, many poets just could not be made to commit
themselves or take a stand on anything.)

I have read with much interest your dialog with Suzuki in
ND #17 — The one point (and very basic it seems to be) upon which
you + he could not make any real rapprochement is that of
affectiveness which you return to in rebuttal and insist upon if I
am not mistaken — of course I am not qualified to evaluate
your arguments in this matter — but it seems to me that the
statement (on page 96) differentiating (1) the affective, personal + dualistic
and (2) the non-affective, non-personal + non-dualistic — is about the
nub of the matter and cannot be talked away no matter

Thank you for the revised version of ORIGINAL CHILD BOMB
I am looking forward to its appearance in Lax's PAX

Reproduction of letter from Ferlinghetti to Merton, 1961.

...much good will on either side. Perhaps another expression of this is in Coomeraswami's observation that the great essential difference between Christian and Oriental art is in the expression in the *faces* depicted in the paintings or statues = the Christian faces having a particularized individualized human *expression* and the Oriental having always the non-individualized, (anonymous?), expression.

(These are not the words he used but this distinction really embodies the same distinction, I think, as that made by Suzuki between Zen and Christianity.)

Coomeraswami I think placed emphasis on the *feeling* or *sentiment* portrayed in the Christian statuary faces in contrast to the absence of this in the Oriental art faces.

If Buddha had been strung on a cross, instead of "eternally sitting there", would he have finally betrayed any 'sentiment' in his face?

Best Salutations, as ever — Lawrence Ferlinghetti

this is in Koomeraswami's[32] observation that the great essential difference between Christian and Oriental art is in the expression on the faces depicted in the paintings or statues – the Christian faces having a particularized individualized human expression and the Oriental having always the non-individualized, (anonymous?), expression. (These are not the words he used but – this distinction really embodies the same distinction, I think, as that made by Suzuki between Zen and Christianity.) Koomeraswami I think placed emphasis on the feeling or sentiment portrayed in the Christian statuary faces in contrast to the absence of this in the Oriental art faces. If Buddha had been strung on a Cross, instead of "eternally sitting there", would he have finally betrayed any 'sentiment' in his face?

Greetings and salutation, as ever –

Lawrence (Ferlinghetti)

P.S. Am sending this via Laughlin, since I thought he might be interested in my reaction to yours in ND #17. Hope you don't mind.

Thank you for the revised version of Original Child Bomb. I am looking forward to its appearance in Lax's PAX.

Ferlinghetti's contribution to the Journal had been a prose/poem called "Picturesque Haiti," which he had written at the very end of 1960 on a visit to the Caribbean. He was shocked by the tremendous poverty he saw there and thought that a photographer ought to "take pictures of the real 'picturesque' island life – for the tourists – shit, hunger, and pissing death – rags and broken shoes – kids with pieces of men's shoes tied to their feet, open sewers seething with revolution," instead

---

[32] Ananda Kentish Coomaraswamy (1877-1947) was an early scholar of Indian art and culture.

of the beautiful sandy beaches and swaying palm trees. He felt that the irony was summed up by their coins which were minted with the slogan "Liberté, Égalité, Fraternité" even though the majority of people were desperately poor. A very small percentage of the population owned everything and that struck Lawrence as more obscene than anything he had seen in the world.

PICTURESQUE HAITI

Port-Au-Prince – There was this girl with the pure sex look who sold people on a rack. She was tall, mulatto, stood beside her rack with its people hung on it, on hangers, like so many pants and dresses swaying, each person with a string attached, somewhere, which the Girl with the Pure Sex Look pulled, to make that person act the way she wanted that Person to act. She jiggled the long string (which was so long it gave the illusion of real Freedom, Equality and Fraternity), causing different looks to come on the faces and on the bodies of those dark inhabitants to which strings were attached. Everyone in the world had some string attached. The Girl with the Pure Sex Look had no visible string attached to herself. She squatted behind her rack and pissed. A string of water attached. ... Her rack was the great Iron Market of Port-au-Prince, casbah of the Caribbean, this Iron Market an enormous native *mercado* (as in Guadalajara, La Paz, Cuzco, any Indian town) – a whole city block of death and dung and pissing desperation, an Exposition of it, everyone on their own hunger-hanger. Some Desolation Photographer should come and do a real Death Magazine job on this Market of Iron, huge hive aswarm with obsidian natives, all hawking, puling, pulling at you, running after you with wares, shouting, crying, laughing, eating and smoking strange leaves. Take picturesque postcard photos of stringbean children with rubbertire shards tied to feet, the Iron Market building itself open on all sides, arcades choked with gypsy encampments of vendors and families, babies and hags squatted among burlap bundles, like voyagers at some end-of-the-world station or Third Avenue Elevated terminal fallen into jungle, a Meccano Erector set, all girders and iron plates bolted together and hung on castiron columns with twin Victorian Gothic iron towers over all like clanking sentry stations on iron prisons... the iron death... weird Reaper with a scythe on those battlements above (Let none escape!): if He had any flesh on him here, would it be White or Black? Those who are starving, some Consul said, still have the strength to dig their own graves.

II.

But it's a beautiful tropical island, really. There's the *Champ de Mars* – huge empty park with concrete shell bandstand with loudspeakers blaring government speeches and martial music all day. From a distance you'd think a great celebration were in progress, great crowds gathered there – only, upon approaching you find no one at all in the great park – at least this season. It's now forbidden to congregate there, last night people were shot walking across it, martial law's in effect, schools have closed, students on strike against the government, the legislature suspended, the Catholic bishop thrown out of the country, the U.S. ambassador temporarily "on leave" in the States. The coins all read Liberté, Égalité, Fraternité. These noble savages are all absolutely equal, except for the 6 percent that owns everything not owned by foreigners. If money's the blood of the poor, in the Port of the Prince the blood has black corpuscles. The Prince has long since washed his hands of it... Ah but – our guidebook tells us – "Tourists beset by beggars, fresh children, arrogant young men and petty thieves in Port-au-Prince will do well to remember that the first and last belong to the declassed riffraff found in any large city, and the others are insecure members of a rising and still-unaccepted middle-class." Our guidebook is written by a noted American poet. It goes on to say that the average cash income of the Haitian is under seventy-five dollars a year. But we can skip this part, our guidebook tells us: "The reader who comes to Haiti to enjoy himself... can be grateful that everything related to the 'dismal science' of economics has been relegated to one chapter – where he is at liberty to skip it."

Happiness Waits for You in
HAITI
Unique in the Caribbean
and All the World

So reads the Tourist Card of Identity issued by the Republic of Haiti, costing two dollars and good for two consecutive years. (But am *I* good for two years of *it?*) A real tropical paradise (even better than Bolivia where the population still craps in the streets). Here we have truly unique living conditions, unique childlike native women still available for only sixty cents (American money), colorful happy natives dancing innocent voodoo dances. Voodoo versus the Catholic Church: as a primitive form of Christianity, voodoo serves its purpose here, its gods made to dance on strings. ...

III.

They are shooting in the *Champ de Mars* this morning. In front of the Presidential Palace some "gaily-uniformed" troops are parading, with fixed bayonets. Out in the *Champ de Mars* from time to time you can hear the dull *whack-whack* of bullets hitting the pavement. Then all is quiet, as if nothing had ever happened, the soldiers disappeared the great white tropical sun burns toward noon. Bands of black kids are out in the park now, after all, sun and bullets don't stop them, they're indomitable, there's always more where they came from, yaws in their feet ("a historic disease of Haiti, contagious as syphilis and having many analogies with it"). Here comes a whole horde of them across the park, chasing a tall, ragged scarecrow of a figure – a mardi gras carnival figure – they're ragging him but they're scared to death of him and they scatter – it's *Baron Samedi,* Voodoo god, always dressed in black, always *hungry*, here He comes, Baron Saturday, carrying a cross, a huge black iron cross he carries askew, dressed in black with a black mask, very tall, smoking a black cigar and wearing dark glasses, through the park at high noon, tilted forward in a lurching walk, as if dragged from above by marionette strings,

68

a death rattle in his throat. He's the Voodoo hunger and death, the yawfeet flee before him, and the herd of flapping feet lead through the *Museum of Primitives* (where its director mumbles in passing, "A revolution won't help them!") and the herd of feet bleats onward and into the Episcopal Cathedral, famous for its murals by Catholic and Protestant primitive painters, and the floor of the cathedral suddenly filled with ulcerous children's feet running from Baron Hunger, more crowding in all the time, the tide of bare yawfeet rising up the walls and over the murals of the Virgin and the Assumption and the flying angels on the ceiling, the flesh of all the figures in the murals turned into knots of bare feet, Christ a black skeleton picked clean, dangling of his Cross like a marionette.

IV.

Pétionville by *camionette* (a jitney, a group taxi) late in the hot afternoon. The half hour ride above the main casbah city costs ten cents. A shaded steep paved road winds up. You catch views between tropic trees, looking back and down, of masts and sails and cracked *quais* of the port. In this town you'll find some pretty fine clubs, for foreigners and the Haitian elite. In this town there's a fine *Club Arabe* on the Place, below low hills where nestle modernist private mansions. There's a funeral just coming up to the Church (of course there's a church on the square) – a black hearse followed by a long black shadow of mourners on foot. "Must be someone important," I say to a little black girl who just happens to be standing around. She answers: "Oui, tous les morts sont importants pour quelques instants, chaque a son petit moment d'importance –" ("Yes, all the dead are important for a few moments, each has his little moment of importance–") It's a curious, grave voice issuing from such a little girl, no more than four feet tall, no more than fourteen. She almost curtsies picturesquely, introduces herself. Her name is Marie, her eyes as grave as her voice. The whites of her eyes are not white but pinkish-brown. Her black hair is wound tight around her head in braids, with little pigtails sticking out. She's got good shoes, too big for her, with enormous rubber soles. she's got a nice skirt and white blouse – a proper Little Person, also with string attached – It turns out it's not just by chance she happens to be hanging around the Place when the *camionette* arrives – It's part of her work at the Sunshine Home to go to the square everyday and pick up tourists and lead them to her orphanage. She leads the way, with a peculiar springy step, down dirt streets with ruts two feet deep. The Sunshine Home is a concrete block house, about the size of a one-family tract home in the States, set beside a mud road in a mud field. There's maybe six rooms altogether, stacked with iron bedsteads to the ceiling – no mattresses – several dozen mostly naked babies and infants of all sizes wandering around – no furniture but the bedsteads – no stove or icebox in the kitchen – there's a wood fire on the cement floor, with kids poking things into it – no grownups in sight – ten-year-old girls nursing one-year-old babies, with pacifiers – the babies have swollen stomachs – smell of sweat and flies and ? – "Mother" is Mrs. Doris Burke, old gaunt Negro woman from Jamaica – they've got photo of her in bird's nest hat – She's out at the moment but Marie gets all the kids posed together on cement front porch, standing skinny and sad, to sing a *bon voyage* song for the American visitor who's sure to send shoes. During the singing, an old man resembling Gandhi stumps by in the dusk of the road, carrying his father on his back. ...

V.

Still, in a place like this, one should disbelieve about 85 percent of what one sees or hears, and check the spelling of the other 15 percent. That's a good foreign correspondent. Things really couldn't be as picturesque as all that. ... Let us return to our hotel. The Park Hotel, even at the height of the tourist season, is a very non-tourist hotel. (It happens there aren't any tourists at the height of this season – all scared away by the political situation, across the Windward Passage from Cuba – someone's going to break wind very soon. And it'll blow through this island in an hour, including the Dominican Republic.) The Hotel du Parc, on the upper edge of the *Champ de Mars*, is a pension. The *pensionnaires* are either cast-up French colonialists (like the *patron* and his bulbous wife-with-concierge-tongue, and the old fat Balzac couples whose tables are in the same corner of the dining room as the *patron's*) or black Haitian civil servants and mulatto *fonctionnaires* (like the head of the Haitian-American Institute, who looks like some U.N. delegate from India) or American residents (a "businessman" from Miami, an English teacher, a soil engineer with hookworm face, a geologist on a project to find drinking water in the hills).

... In the night of the winter of 1960-61, after the usual five-course family dinner, this strange cargo sits rocking in separate chairs on the front veranda, looking out into the dense cricket vegetation of the courtyard through which still filters martial music from the now totally black *Champ de Mars*. I am advised not to venture out there at this hour. The speaker is Leo the Lip. Leo the Lip is several saints in one act, if you take him at face value. Leo the Lip has a face from a very common coinage. It is only the eyes that stamp that face with value. It is a high-domed Jew-face, such as you may see walking through the Clothing District or on Miami's beach any day. Leo the Lip claims to be a millionaire. Leo the Lip's mother, a Polish immigrant, "battled her way out of the ghetto" (he tells me). Leo the Lip did the same, out of Jersey City. Now, totally bald, fat with meat lips, forty-eight years old, he's rich after buying Miami land at a few dollars an acre, said land now being nothing but the Miami Airport. Now he runs horses at various tracks, speculates in overseas crops (strawberries in Haiti), reads geopolitics, conceptual philosophy, visionary poetry. Been married "many times" (he tells me), now doesn't know where to go, what to do with himself anymore, feels himself too old to make a home anywhere again, though he has two plush houses, one in Miami, one in Santa Barbara. When he talks his great, longing eyes are a long way from the meat lips, raising his long white bullface out of the Life of Eat and Shit – his gaze is somewhere out over the bougainvillea in the Haitian dark. He's on the side of the Haitians, loaded with all kinds of fascinating, weird info on everyone on the island, a kind of walking, farting U.S. Information Service in reverse. Leo the Lip is heated up, at the moment, about

71

Ugly American from World Bank who's just been down here "insulting the natives" – addressing Haitian agricultural experts and economists as if they were illiterate children, talking down to a commission of them, speaking neither of their languages (French, Creole), understanding nothing but Pure American – Leo the Lip's telling me all this on the dark porch of this life – everyone hung there together in the night, rocking and nodding – A loud wind that came up, clacking the palm branches, has suddenly died down – Leo the Lip stops short, aware of everyone listening. I'm composing a poem in my head, which I hope will turn out Revolutionary. After a long time rocking (rapidly, as if a string were attached) Leo the Lip says to me: "The residue of time is compassion." He looks around at the other cast-up earth-passengers, still rocking, not about to leave this ark in the dangerous night, prisoners of history. ... *Loose leaves and aeroplanes blow away on the wind, in what they call Freedom.*

Just as he thought, Merton was criticized by his superiors for contributing to *The Journal For The Protection of All Beings*, as his following letter indicates. The title alone must have caused his administrators to raise an eyebrow and even though they might have agreed with the sentiments of some of the writers, they decided that maybe Merton shouldn't contribute anything more to future issues. As always, Merton agreed to obey them and wrote to J Laughlin saying "one principle I have to work on at the moment is to remain dissociated from any and every group whatever, including Catholic ones if possible. Just to appear on my own in odd places and when occasion demands, especially when it is a question of statements like this... They should be made in the air, so to speak, without any connection with anybody else's statements. Hence I cannot get into any protest group. Much as I sympathize and much as I would enjoy doing so. I liked Ferlinghetti's long Cuba poem and other material in that connection." Still, over the next year Merton was able to devise a way to get his voice of protest heard. That culminated in a series of writings that became known as the "Cold War Letters," which Laughlin distributed widely. The letter also highlights Merton's own growing interest in Buddhism and Eastern philosophies.

Dec 12, 1961
Dear Lawrence:

J forwarded your letter to me, and I am sorry to hear that you have been sick. All my friends have been in hospitals, operated on, diagnosed as about to die, God alone knows what. We are all cashing in our chips, so it seems, except that for my part I am still standing, though hungry.

About the *Journal*: don't think I was personally embarrassed by it. But as I rather expected, Fr Abbot took a good look at it and decided that from now on I am not to contribute any more to it. That is the only thing I regret. I admit that I am not much dazzled by the approach most of the writers take. I mean I can get along from page to page without getting swept off my feet with enthusiasm. Not that I am mad at dirty words, they are perfectly good honest words as far as I am concerned, and they form part of my own interior mumblings a lot of the time, why not? I just wonder if this isn't another kind of jargon which is a bit more respectable than the jargon of the slick magazines, but not very much more. And I wonder just how much is actually <u>said</u> by it.

However that is not what I mean, because I thought a lot of the stuff was real good, like especially the one about David Meltzer's baby getting born.[33] This was fine. And a lot of good in the Robt Duncan,[34] which I liked mostly. I liked very much your beautiful Haiti[35] and best thing in the whole book was Nez Percé.[36] So there. I haven't read the Camus[37] yet but him I like always. Yet I don't think it was what one might have expected, as a lot of the material was not very near the target, <u>and I am inclined to doubt the reality of the moral concern of a lot of these people who are articulate</u> about the question of war in your *Journal*. And I think that is one reason why you can't get the other ones to commit themselves. I don't know if there is anything they are apt to mean about a problem as big as this. However, they are all much more human and more real than the zombies who have all kinds of facts about deterrence and finite deterrence and all out non-survivability and all in first strike ballistic preemption plus as distinguished from massive plus plus retaliation plus.

---

[33] Meltzer's poem was entitled "Journal of the Birth."

[34] Duncan's poem was entitled "Properties and Our Real Estate."

[35] Reference here to Ferlinghetti's prose piece, "Picturesque Haiti."

[36] Chief Joseph's famous surrender statement, "I will fight no more forever."

[37] Albert Camus' contribution was "The Artist As Symbol of Freedom."

74

As regards the Christianity Buddhism thing: both Suzuki and I ended up hanging in various trees among the birds nests. I am not insisting upon anything, least of all affectivity. That remark was a journalistic kind of remark, referring to the way Christianity and Buddhism look to people who are very definite about being one or the other and very sure that the metaphysic of one excludes the metaphysic of the other. This is all probably quite so. But Zen is beyond metaphysics and so, as far as I am concerned, is the kind of Christian experience that seems to me most relevant, and which is found in Eckhart[38] and the Rhenish mystics and all the mystics for that matter. I agree theoretically that there is a complete division between the two approaches: one personalistic, dualistic, etc. the other non-dualistic. Only trouble is that Suzuki's very distinction between God and Godhead is dualistic, and his lineup of Buddha vs Christ is also dualistic, and when he starts that he forgets his Zen. So he forgets his Zen. He can forget his Zen too if he wants to or has to, no law saying you have to remember your Zen every minute of the day. It seems to me the Cross says just as much about Zen, or just as little, as the serene face of the Buddha. Of course the historic, medieval concern with the expression of feeling and love in the Crucified Christ is nowhere near Zen, it is Bakhti [Bhakti] or however you spell it, and that is another matter. But essentially the Crucifix is a non-image, a destroyed image, a wiped out image, a nothing, an annihilation. It just depends what you are looking at and who you are that looks at it. So the Zens say burn all the Buddhas, and they come out with the same

---

[38] Meister Eckhart was a 14th century German theologian.

thing in the end, as far as the destruction of the image is concerned.

What I do think matters is liberty. The complete freedom and unlimited, unrestricted quality of love, not its affectivity. This I think the Zens are after in their own way too, though more intellectual about it. And note that Zen is full of affectivity too, look at the Zen paintings: plenty compassion, humor, comment, all sorts stuff which in the west we would frown at calling it literature.

Well, this I have to stop, and put into the box. I enclose a stuffy sort of article, which will probably be in *Jubilee*.[39] And God bless you, all kinds of happiness at Christmas and any other time too.

As ever, in Christ
Tom

***

From the next few years, little correspondence between the two remains. Another issue of the *Journal* was published, but as Lawrence mentioned earlier, he was not as active in its publication. J Laughlin kept each of them informed about the work of the other and continued to send new books to Merton on a regular basis. Still, the two poets never met. One of the books that J did send to Merton was Allen Ginsberg's *Kaddish and Other Poems*, which William Carlos Williams had recommended he read. "I agree with you about it. I think it is great and living poetry and certainly religious in its concern," Thomas wrote in 1961. "In fact, who are more concerned with ultimates than the beats? Why do you think that just because I am a monk I should be likely to shrink from beats? Who am I to shrink from anyone? I am a monk, therefore by definition, as I understand it, the chief friend of the beats and

---

[39] Probably a reference to Merton's article "The General Dance," which appeared in *Jubilee* magazine's Dec. 1961 issue.

one who has not business reproving them. And why should I?" A few years later, Merton's opinion of the beats still hadn't changed. In a letter to Stefan Baciu in 1965, he wrote: "As to the U.S. Beats I am more in sympathy with them but in most cases I do not respond to them fully."

Ginsberg was also interested in Merton's response to "Kaddish," the long poem which many think is Allen's greatest. Not long after Ginsberg heard that J had sent Merton a copy of the poem, he asked, "I would like to know, what Merton's reaction to Kaddish is – for that matter I wonder what he thought of Howl, if he saw it." Laughlin did not immediately answer Allen's question and so Allen mentioned it again in his next letter. "Saw your remarks re Merton in letter to Gregory [Corso] and was fascinated by possibility that he [Merton] had not ever actually experienced some breakthrough visionary state – I would be curious his reaction to the Magic Psalm poem in Kaddish since it's practically a catholic type prayer. If you see him again and if he ever sees my book."

After the publication of Merton's poem "Chant to Be Used In Processions Around A Site With Furnaces," the comedian Lenny Bruce adapted it as a routine in his act. Bruce and another comedian, Mort Sahl, were among the first comics since Will Rogers to use what they were reading in newspapers and magazines as a basis for their routines. Bruce employed Merton's poem to point out how little had changed in society since the defeat of the Nazis. As with much of Bruce's act, the routine skirted the borders of what was acceptable to an American audience. Even though much of what he said during his regular act was considered obscene, by using the words of "Chant" he wanted to show people what he felt should really be considered obscene. It never brought tremendous laughs, but it made a point and he continued to make use of it onstage for years.

Near the end of his act, Bruce would call for the spotlight to focus solely on his face as he assumed an exaggerated German accent. "My name is Adolf Eichmann," he would say, making the same incorrect assumption about the narrator of the poem that Ferlinghetti had made, or maybe sensing that more people in his audience were aware of Eichmann than of Rudolf Höss. "The Jews came every day to vat they thought vould be fun in the showers. The mothers were quite ingenious. They vould take the children und hide them in bundles of clothing. Ve found the children, scrubbed them, put them in the chambers and sealed them in." The audience squirmed in their seats. No one knew how to react, exactly the reaction that Bruce wanted to provoke. Weren't these images truly more obscene than his off-color jokes?

Lenny Bruce was already dead by the time Thomas Merton learned about the use of his poem in Lenny's act, but he wasn't upset about it. "What he did was a marvelous adaptation of a much longer and more intricate poem of mine. This was the same poem, but cut down to a series of left hooks for the night club or wherever he did it, and much funnier. My own is very dour and quiet, this is rambunctious and wild." It was exactly the kind of social comment that Merton thought was needed during the Vietnam War era lest we repeat the sins.

Merton felt a need to be a part of the world's struggle for peace and love on the planet, but at the same time he desired to be left alone to meditate. Eventually, at his request, he was assigned to a hermitage on the monastery grounds, where he would be isolated and free to pursue his own thoughts without interruption. In 1968, he even began to publish a magazine of his own called *Monks Pond,* which included contributions by Beat poets like Gary Snyder. Even Jack Kerouac submitted two poems for the second issue. After nearly three years of living alone in the woods behind the monastery, Merton felt that he was not isolated enough. He began to dream about finding a new retreat, even more isolated, where he might live alone in pursuit of his twin devotions; to worship God and to write.

To that end, he asked his superiors for permission to visit two other monasteries, one in California and one in New Mexico, where he thought he might find more seclusion and where he hoped to escape the daily duties he had at Gethsemani Abbey. They agreed that he could travel to see each location before making any decision. First, he would visit California and then go on to New Mexico. Between the two stops, he planned to take advantage of the opportunity to lay over in San Francisco and visit Ferlinghetti for the first time. When he mentioned this possibility to Lawrence, he discovered that City Lights had a spare room on the floor above the publishing company's offices on the corner of Grant and Filbert, which they occasionally lent to visiting writers for a day or two. It would be the first and only time the two poets ever met.

1968 turned out to be one of the most tragic years in American history. In early April, the great civil rights leader, Martin Luther King Jr., was assassinated in Memphis. The U.S. military involvement in Vietnam's civil war continued to grow and the resulting mass protests began to tear the country apart. At the time of Merton's visit to California, no one knew that Robert Kennedy would also be shot and killed that year or that Merton himself would die in a freak accident. As it was, Merton was looking forward to his trip as a chance to explore a bit of the country he hadn't seen before. With any luck he might even discover a place where he could live in more seclusion than in his little shack in Kentucky. His plan was laid out. He would visit Our Lady of the Redwoods Abbey, a Cistercian convent in Whitethorn, CA, a few hours north of San Francisco. Then, after a short visit there, he would drive back to San Francisco to stay with Ferlinghetti before flying to Abiquiu, New Mexico to visit a Benedictine monastery there called Christ in the Desert.

On May 6, 1968, Merton's flight from Chicago touched down in San Francisco and he stopped off in the airport lounge to have a couple of daiquiris before getting on the tiny airplane for the flight to Eureka. From there, people from the Redwoods Abbey drove him up for the next week's stay. Everything seemed different in California. The enormous redwoods were quite a contrast with the smaller trees he knew so well in Kentucky and he imagined that he would never be able to live anywhere but here. The trees made him feel that he was sheltered in a living cathedral. The nuns at the convent found an isolated house for him at Bear Harbor and he immediately felt relaxed and at home. He talked to the owner of the property and made inquiries about renting the cabin for a long-term retreat.

On May 15, he left to continue on his journey to inspect the monastery in New Mexico, although by then he thought that living anywhere except in the redwood forest would be a mistake. Two nuns drove him into San Francisco and once he got there Merton called Ferlinghetti from a pay phone. Lawrence was out doing some errands at the time, but they stopped into City Lights before going to dinner and left a message for him. At the bookstore, Merton bought books by the T'ang poets, William Carlos Williams' *Kora In Hell*, and a collection of poems by Sven Heilo, a law student from Sweden with whom Merton had been corresponding. From there, they went to an Italian restaurant called Polo's, where Ferlinghetti met them. After a bottle of chianti, the conversation grew warmer and Lawrence and Tom went off to the Caffe Trieste, a neighborhood espresso place on Grant Avenue. There "a young musician told of some visions he had had. Good visions and not on drugs either," Merton said. Ferlinghetti remembered quite vividly that although they talked about literature, no attractive woman passed by the window without Tom's notice.

At the end of the evening, Lawrence took Merton over to the apartment half-way up Telegraph Hill at 485 Filbert Street where he was to sleep. It was a comfortable place that Lawrence himself had lived in for a few years before they began to host the occasional visiting author. Notable writers like Andrei Voznesensky, Charles Bukowski, and of course Allen Ginsberg had all stayed there from time to time. Merton noted that there were posters in the stairway of the cover of René Daumal's novel, *Mount Analogue*, which he wanted to read. Inside, he found a wide range of books to look at including a "good collection of H.M. Engensbuyer's verse," which Tom said he read in the morning while waiting for the nuns to pick him up. The apartment also had a typewriter on which the guests could compose poetry if the mood hit them. Merton, who had been practicing photography, took a few pictures of the typewriter and the view from the windows. In his diary, he noted "The buildings of San Francisco, the two-spired church in North Beach, the apartments and streets of

View from Ferlinghetti's window, 1968.

Ferlinghetti's typewriter and desk, 1968. Photographs by Thomas Merton. Used with Permission of the Merton Legacy Trust and the Thomas Merton Center at Bellarmine University.

Telegraph Hill in warm, pale, South American or desert colors – snake colors, but charming and restful. Pretty as Havana and less noisy, though there was plenty of motor noise at night with cars climbing those steep hills."

Unfortunately, the windows overlooked noisy Grant Avenue, which kept Tom awake much of the night. After 26 years spent in a quiet monastery in the woods, the roar of cars in the city at night disturbed his sleep on the mattress which was stretched out on the floor. He noticed a guitar and a tape recorder next to a window that opened onto the fire escape. It wasn't until around 1:30 in the morning that he was finally able to drift off to sleep for a few hours, before the garbage trucks started their rounds.

Merton continued to make notes in his journal the next morning:

> In the little Italian restaurant in the North Beach area where I had an early breakfast today, a Chinese man, looking as though bewildered with drugs or something, ate repeated orders of macaroni with bottles of beer. It was seven o'clock in the morning. Much comment in Italian by the staff and the patrons. One of the hatted Italians whirled his finger next to the temple and pointed to the man, 'you're crazy.'

Lawrence recalled that he drove Merton to the airport that day and saw him off on the next leg of his trip. On the flight to New Mexico, Tom read Han Yu's poems in the book of T'ang poetry that he had purchased the day before at City Lights Bookstore. After a few days at the monastery in Abiquiu, which he found nearly as remarkable as the one in the redwood forest, he flew back to Kentucky via Dallas, Memphis, Nashville, and Louisville, reading the copy of Daumal's *Mount Analogue* that Ferlinghetti had given him before his departure. He found it to be "a very fine book" and impressed him so much that he excerpted bits of it in his journal.

By May 21, he had arrived back in his hermitage at

Gethsemani, where he continued to think about his long-term plans for the future. He finally decided, at least for a time, that after his upcoming trip to Asia, he would return to California and live at Bear Harbor. "It is not right that I should die under lesser trees," he wrote to himself. Later he said, "I need the sound of those waves, that desolation, that emptiness."

While in San Francisco, Ferlinghetti and Merton had talked about Walter Evans-Wentz, whose translation of the *Tibetan Book of the Dead* was becoming all the rage with a new generation of spiritual seekers. Hippies were fast replacing beatniks in American cities and their interest in everything exotic was exciting to both Tom and Lawrence. Although Evans-Wentz had died in 1965, his secretary was someone who Merton had been in touch with and Ferlinghetti wanted to talk to him about the possibility of working with unpublished manuscripts. He wrote a short note asking Tom for his address.

29 May 68
Dear Tom – Greetings. ....
    If you have the name and address of that Evans-Wentz man[40] – (the one with the E-W material) – I'd appreciate your sending it to me.... Hope you had a high trip home –
    Yrs -
    Lawrence F.

June 5, 1968
Dear Lawrence:
    The former secretary of Evans Wentz is Louis Blevins, of Box 701, Encinitas, Cal. 92024, which ought to be somewhere near you. He says he has a lot of material. If I get a

---

[40] Walter Evans-Wentz (1878-1965) was a scholar of Tibetan Buddhism and translated *The Tibetan Book of the Dead* in 1927.

chance I'll tell him you will contact him.

Thanks very much for the contribution for MPOND.[41] I sent some more yesterday or the day before. Hope they reach you all right. And don't forget — send me something of yours if you can, and urge others to. Only problem is the four letter words, on account of the monks in the print shop.

I very much liked *MOUNT ANALOGUE*. A great idea. Too bad he did not get further with it. But an impressive book. The Sufi man I told you of, Raza Arasteh, has a piece in MPOND II.[42] It will give you an idea. The longer version of that piece and another article like it might make a pamphlet for you. I told him to send you his book, but I guess it's too long for you and would require too much editing.

The monastery I went to in New Mexico is a very good spot, in the Chamas [Chama] Canyon.[43] Lots of Indian stuff around. I like Santa Fe, too.

Thanks for putting me up at City Lights. Felt a bit like the old days. I enjoyed looking out in the morning on a street like Havana, full of pretty little Chinese kids going to school. It was good meeting you. Bellarmine College here is probably going to contact you about a reading some time later in the year.

My best always,
Tom

---

[41] Merton published four issues of a little magazine called *Monks Pond* that year.

[42] Reza Arasteh's "The Art of Rebirth" appeared in the second issue of *Monks Pond* in 1968.

[43] The Monastery of Christ in the Desert is a Roman Catholic Benedictine monastery founded in 1964.

Merton had replied quickly from Kentucky, but sadly that very evening Robert Kennedy would be assassinated in California while campaigning for the Presidency. Tom grieved for the Kennedy family and felt that "it seems to be another step toward degradation and totalism on the part of the whole country. It will be used as an excuse for tightening up police control... to silence protest and jail non-conformists. ... The situation seems to me very grave."

In August, Merton was scheduled to go to Washington DC for a speaking engagement and while waiting for his plane he ate in the airport's Luau room and then hung around the bar reading Ferlinghetti's newest collection of plays called *Routines*. On September 10, 1968, he left Kentucky once more to attend an Apache festival. By September 26, he was on his way to Alaska before flying to Santa Barbara where he was to speak at a conference at the Center for the Study of Democratic Institutions. It was a lot of traveling and public speaking for a man who wanted to live in a hermitage and retreat from the world in order to pray and meditate, but once celebrity had him in its clutches it would not let him go. The high point of this western trip was that he was permitted to stay once again at the Redwoods monastery, where he felt he could find the true peace and isolation he craved. Then on October 15, he began his extended journey to Asia.

The purpose of the trip was three-fold. Merton had been invited to give lectures and talks at various religious meetings and retreats, but he was also interested in meeting the leaders of Eastern religions, especially Buddhists, who were far advanced in the practice of meditation. He felt he had much to learn from them. The trip would also give him an opportunity to get away from his duties at home and to weigh the merits of each of the refuges he had visited over the past six months. At this point, he was ready to settle down somewhere for the rest of his life. Secretly that was his main reason for this trip.

After touching down in Bangkok, where he was able to lighten his load of heavy baggage, he flew on to India. While he was staying at the grand Oberoi Hotel in Calcutta, he wrote to Ferlinghetti about a chance meeting he had with a Tibetan teacher. The person that Merton had found so interesting was named Chögyam Trungpa Rinpoche. In his book, *A Nontheist's Journey,* the author Rob Lee describes the meeting of the two spiritual leaders.

> This was a very improbable crossing of paths. Neither had previously known anything about the other, and they had no intention of meeting. Thomas Merton was far away from his Kentucky monastery for the first time since he entered it in 1941. Trungpa had left Asia in 1963 to study at Oxford and teach in the West, and was making his last brief visit to India. They met by chance in the lobby of the hotel, shared drinks together in Trungpa's suite, conversed intensely about their lives and spiritual practices, became true friends, and planned to meet the next year to co-write a book that would compare and perhaps reconcile Christian and Buddhist spirituality.

It was another of those intersecting coincidences that Merton had with the Beat Generation.

Chögyam Trungpa Rinpoche was born in Tibet in 1939 and had escaped from the Chinese takeover at the age of twenty-one. He was the lineage holder of both the Kagyu and Nyingma traditions of Tibetan Buddhism, and a supreme abbot of a long line of scholars that stretched back centuries. He had settled in the United Kingdom but, like Merton, was taking a break. After his retreat at Taktsang in Bhutan, where he received the Sadhana of Mahamudra, he travelled for a few months in India and it was there that he chanced to meet Merton. Later, he settled in the U.S. to lecture and establish a series of schools for the purpose of teaching the practice of the Vajrayana. In 1971, Allen Ginsberg became one of his meditation students and a few years later Ginsberg helped Trungpa establish the Naropa Institute, where Allen taught until his own death in 1997. Many Beat writers became students of Trungpa including Diane di Prima, Anne

Chögyam Trungpa Rinpoche. Copyright Allen Ginsberg Estate.

Waldman, and Peter Orlovsky and, almost without exception, all of the Beats at one time or another taught at Naropa at the request of Ginsberg who became the director of the Jack Kerouac School of Disembodied Poetics, as the literature department of Naropa was called. All of this was unknown to Merton and Ferlinghetti at the time of course.

Oct 18. 1968
Dear Larry –
    I am suggesting to a friend of mine, a Tibetan Lama, that he might send you a manuscript he is preparing. It is of great interest, a contemporary document in the authentic Tibetan tradition and first rate. The English may need a little improvement but the material is as impressive as the *Tibetan Book of the Dead*. The author's name is Trungpa Rinpoche. I am giving him City Lights' address and he will contact you some time.

I am over here on an extended trip & hope to keep extending it....

My very best

Tom Merton.

(You can always reach me through Gethsemani – mark for forwarding.)

In his own journal, Merton noted the meeting in more detail:

> Yesterday, quite by chance, I met Chögyam Trungpa Rinpoche and his secretary, a nice young Englishman whose Tibetan name is Kunga. Today I had lunch with them and talked about going to Bhutan. But the important thing is that we are people who have been waiting to meet for a long time. Chögyam Trungpa is a completely marvelous person. Young, natural, without front or artifice, deep, awake, wise. I am sure we will be seeing a lot more of each other, whether around northern India and Sikkim or in Scotland, where I am now determined to go to see his Tibetan monastery if I can.

It was also a meeting important enough to be long remembered by Trungpa. Years later, he recalled their meeting:

> Father Merton's visit to Southeast Asia took place when I was in Calcutta.... I had the feeling that I was meeting an old friend, a genuine friend. In fact, we planned to work on a book containing selections from the sacred writings of Christianity and Buddhism. We planned to meet either in Great Britain or in North America. He was the first genuine person I met from the West. After meeting Thomas Merton, I visited several monasteries in Great Britain, and at some of them I was asked to give talks on meditation, which I

Photograph of Thomas Merton and the Dalai Lama, Nov. 1968. Used with Permission of the Merton Legacy Trust and the Thomas Merton Center at Bellarmine University.

did.... I was very impressed and moved by the contemplative aspect of Christianity, and by the monasteries themselves. Their lifestyle and the way they conducted themselves convinced me that the only way to join the Christian tradition and the Buddhist tradition together is by means of bringing together Christian contemplative practice with Buddhist meditative practice.

From Calcutta, at the beginning of November 1968, Merton went on to Dharamsala, where he was introduced to the 33-year-old Dalai Lama. The two religious leaders got along well and Merton found the Buddhist monk "energetic, generous, and warm." Then Merton flew to Sri Lanka to explore the sacred shrines and temples there before heading to Bangkok, Thailand, where he was expected to speak to a group of Asian Benedictines and Cistercians at a convention of the Red Cross. After giving a lecture on the morning of December 10, 1968, he returned to his room and took a bath. By accident, he touched a fan that had faulty wiring and died

89

suddenly from a massive electric shock. His body was flown back to the United States on a military plane that was bringing home the bodies of servicemen who had died fighting the war in Vietnam, the war Merton had spent so much energy protesting against. He was buried in the cemetery of his home of twenty-five years, Gethsemani Abbey.

So in the end, Ferlinghetti wasn't the last person to see Merton off on his trip to Asia, but over the years the story changed with the retelling and became one of Lawrence's favorite memories. Lawrence lived for more than fifty years following Merton's death, but he never forgot him or his message of peace and love. He continued to invoke the spirit of Thomas Merton in his later poetry. In 1993, he wrote a poem entitled "A Buddha in the Woodpile" based on the tragic killing in Waco, Texas, of a group of religious extremists called the Branch Davidians by government agents. Lawrence included Merton in a list of people who might have been able to stop the slaughter that day.

A BUDDHA IN THE WOODPILE

If there had been only
one Buddhist in the woodpile
In Waco Texas
to teach us how to sit still
one saffron Buddhist in the back rooms
just one Tibetan lama
just one Taoist
just one Zen
just one Thomas Merton Trappist
just one saint in the wilderness
of Waco USA
.....

Then that sick cult and its children
might still be breathing
the free American air
of the First Amendment

And even as late as 2001 in his poem "Mouth," Lawrence was musing that "Perhaps I'll join the Trappists" in order to learn to stop talking so much about nonsense.

And who knows
maybe someday
it'll break right open
and blurt right out
some great poetry
in some primal tongue
made of love and light and dung
some great immortal song
no human ever heard before
nor ever sung

Ferlinghetti passed away on February 22, 2021, just a month shy of his 102nd birthday. One of the things that made the two writers kindred spirits was that they were both searching for something beyond their everyday existence. They were seeking purity of heart and clarity of vision. Both tried to find an authentic way of existing in the modern world and each lived a life filled with paradoxes. One man left an urban intellectual career for a life of rural retreat only to be drawn back into the realm of international fame and debate; the other accidentally fell into the world of publishing and became one of America's intellectual giants. He shaped the literature of the twentieth century, while continually dreaming of escaping it all to pursue his own flow of ideas.

BIBLIOGRAPHY

Aquilina, Mike. "Original Hipsters: the Beats' Catholic
 Confusion." (2019) [online]

Baciu, Stefan. "Latin America and Spain in the Poetic World
 of Thomas Merton." pp. 13-28.

Belcastro, David. "Thomas Merton and the Beat
 Generation: A Subterranean Monastic Community" (in)
 Merton Society - Oakham Papers (2002) pp. 79-91.

Blanco, Jose. "Fernando Pessoa's Critical and Editorial
 Fortune in English: A Selective Chronological
 Overview." (in) *Portuguese Studies,* vol. 24, no 2 (2008) pp.
 13-32.

Bree, Germaine. "'New' Poetry and Poets in France and
 the United States", (in) *Wisconsin Studies in Contemporary
 Literature,* vol. 2, no. 2 (Spring-Summer 1961) pp. 5-11.

Cherkovski, Neeli. *Ferlinghetti: A Biography.* Garden City, NY:
 Doubleday, 1979.

Cioffoletti, Beth. "Louie, Louie", (2006) [online]

Collins, John. "'Where Are We Really Going Always Home':
 Thomas Merton and Herman Hesse," (in) *Religion and the
 Arts,* no. 16 (2012) p. 78-99.

Cooper, David D. (ed.) *Thomas Merton and James Laughlin:
 Selected Letters.* NY: W.W. Norton, 1997.

Cunningham, Lawrence S. and others. "Merton at One
 Hundred: Reflections on 'The Seven Storey Mountain'."
 (in) *American Catholic Studies,* vol. 126, no 2 (Summer
 2015) pp. 69-80.

Cunningham, Lawrence. *Thomas Merton and the Monastic*

Vision. Grand Rapids, MI: Wm. B. Eerdmans Pub., 1999, pp. 92-94.

Dart, Ron. "Merton Meets the Beats" (in) *The Pacific Rim Review of Books,* no. 4, (Fall 2006) pp. 25, 34.

Feldman, Matthew. "Thomas Merton: Catholic modernist?" (in) *Textual Practice,* vol. 34, no. 9, pp. 1473-1499. (no date)

Ferlinghetti, Lawrence. *Writing Across the Landscape.* NY: Liveright, 2015.

Fox, Peggy L. "James Laughlin and Thomas Merton: 'Louie, I Think This Is The Beginning Of A Beautiful Friendship'." (in) *The Merton Annual,* vol. 26 (2013) pp. 12-23.

Ginn, Robert. "The Paradox of Solitude: Jack Kerouac and Thomas Merton." (in) *Merton Seasonal,* vol. 24, no. 2 (Summer 1999) pp. 18-26.

Goldfarb, David A. "The Polish Poet: traveler, Exile, Expatriate, World Citizen." *Ulbandus Review,* vol. 7 (2003) pp. 155-173).

Greene, Virginie. "Three Approaches to Poetry." (in) *PMLA,* vol. 120, no. 1 (Jan. 2005) pp. 219-234.

Inchausti, Robert. "Thomas Merton, 'Honorary Beatnik'."

Johnson, Joyce. *The Voice Is All: The Lonely Victory of Jack Kerouac.* NY: Viking, 2012.

Johnston, Paul. "Thomas Merton: 1915-1968" (in) *American Writers,* pp. 193-212.

Keane, James T. "Farewell Lawrence Ferlinghetti, the non-conforming Catholic poet who inspired Bob Dylan and Thomas Merton." (in) *America: The Jesuit Review,* 2021. [online]

Kelly, Richard. "Thomas Merton and Poetic Vitality. *Renascence* (Spring 1960) pp. 139-142+.

Labrie, Ross. "Thomas Merton." (in) *Gale Dictionary of Literary Biography* (1986)

MacNiven, Ian S. "New Directions, Advance Guard

Publishing, and Cover Art. (in) *Archives of American Art Journal,* vol. 52, no. 3-4 (Fall 2013) pp. 40-44.

Merton, Thomas. *A Life in Letters: The Essential Collection.* Notre Dame, IN: Ave Maria Press, 2008.

Merton, Thomas. *The Other Side of the Mountain.* SF: HarperSanFrancisco, 1998.

Merton, Thomas. *The Road to Joy: Letters to New and Old Friends.* NY: Farrar, Straus & Giroux, 1989.

Merton, Thomas. *The Seven Storey Mountain.* NY: Houghton Mifflin Harcourt, 1998.

Merton, Thomas. *Woods, Shore, Desert.* Santa Fe, NM: Museum of New Mexico Press, 1982.

Miller, William D. *A Harsh and Dreadful Love: Dorothy Day and the Catholic Worker Movement.* Garden City, NY: Image, 1974.

Morgan, Ted. *Literary Outlaw: The Life and Times of William S. Burroughs.* NY: Norton, 1988.

Nicosia, Gerald. *Memory Babe.* NY: Penguin, 1986.

Pearson, Paul M. "Poetry of the Sneeze: Thomas Merton and Nicanor Parra." Thomas Merton Society webpage [online]

Pramuk, Christopher. "Contemplation and the Suffering Earth: Thomas Merton, Pope Francis, and the Next Generation. (in) *Open Theology,* vol. 4 (2018), pp. 212-227.

Schumacher, Michael. *Dharma Lion: A Critical Biography of Allen Ginsberg.* NY: St. Martin's Press, 1992.

Silesky, Barry. *Ferlinghetti: The Artist in His Time.* NY: Warner, 1990.

Smelcer, John. "Finding Thomas Merton." (in) *Tikkun,* vol. 32, n. 3 (Summer 2017) pp. 46-51.

Stuart, Angus. "Merton and the Beats". (in) *Thomas Merton: Monk on the Edge,* (ed. by Ross Labrie and Angus Stuart). Vancouver, BC: Thomas Merton Society of Canada, 2012, pp. 79-100.

Stuart, Angus. "Visions of Tom: Jack Kerouac's Monastic

Elder Brother. A Preliminary Exploration." (in) *The Merton Journal*, vol. 8, no 1 (Easter 2001) pp. 40-46.

Wakefield, Dan. "A Memoir of Mark Van Doren." (in) *Ploughshares,* vol. 17, no. 2-3 (Fall 1991) pp. 100-111.

Weis, Monica. "Thomas Merton: Advance Man for New Age Thinking About the Environment." (in) *Interdisciplinary Studies in Literature and Environment,* vol. 5, no. 2 (Summer 1998), pp. 1-7.

Wilkes, Paul (director); Wilkes, Paul and Audrey Laurine Glynn (producers). *Merton: A Film Biography.*

Wilkes, Paul and Gray Matthews. "Interview With Lawrence Ferlinghetti". *The Merton Annual* (2009), pp. 220-226.